MODERN SHAMANIC LIVING

MODERN SHAMANIC LIVING

New Explorations of an Ancient Path

Evelyn C. Rysdyk

SAMUEL WEISER, INC.

York Beach, Maine

First published in 1999 by
Samuel Weiser, Inc.
P. O. Box 612
York Beach, ME 03910-0612
www.weiserbooks.com

Library of Congress Cataloging-in-Publication Data

Rysdyk, Evelyn C.
    Modern shamanic living : new explorations of an ancient
path / Evelyn C. Rysdyk.
       p. cm.
    Includes bibliographical references and index.
    ISBN 1-57863-125-4 (pbk. : alk. paper)
    1. Spiritual life. 2. Shamanism—Miscellanea. 3. Self-
realization—Religious aspects. I. Title.
BL624.R88 1999   99-22633
291.4'4—dc21   CIP

Cover art is "Living in the Magic" by Evelyn C. Rysdyk © 1999
Cover Design by Ed Stevens

BJ

Typeset in 14 pt. Bookman

Printed in the United States of America

08 07 06 05 04 03 02 01 00 99
10 9 8   7   6   5   4   3   2   1

This book is dedicated to my extraordinary partner,
Allie Knowlton, who amazes me by nurturing
ever-deeper relationships with both the
seen and unseen worlds.
Thank you for being in my life.

Table of Contents

Publisher's Note

The self-help suggestions and shamanic techniques described in this book are in no way meant to replace professional medical or mental health assistance. Please consult a medical professional for any persistent condition.

Preface

The character of the hunter/gatherer has, for some time, whispered its urgent appeal into my consciousness. Answering the call has been like taking those final few steps at the beach, when, as I reach the top of the dunes, my eyes are struck by the enormous horizon. The shear space overwhelms my whole being and the sensory overload blows away all ordinary thoughts. This project has had that kind of effect on me.

The hunter/gatherer is the name I have given to an inner part of ourselves that I believe has the abilities we need to really *thrive*. This inner character views all of life with a refreshing perspective that can shift our experience of situations from consternation or emotional pain into one of insight and expansion. It is also a viewpoint that is full of compassion.

I have written this book to introduce you to your own hunter/gatherer. In addition, I have shared some of the wonderful gifts I have received from my own. These gifts extend into every part of my life. They have profoundly changed my relationships with others, my relationship with my community, with the natural world, and especially my relationship with myself. These changes have been joyful, positive, and long-lasting.

The challenge in this work has been to find experiential approaches to the material. For me to try to simply explain this material would have been incomplete, like trying to describe the ocean to someone born in a land-locked state. How do you explain the remarkably complex smell or texture of the sand between your toes? For that reason, each segment of the book contains experiential exercises/questions. I want you to know the hunter/gatherer's perspective from the *inside*. It is my personal belief that, once we really experience a new idea we are less likely to fall back into perceptions that no longer serve us. Our previous paradigms become outmoded and we move ahead.

Therefore, I suggest that, to the best of your ability, you approach this work and the exercises with an open mind. Give yourself permission to enjoy the act of getting to know this part of yourself and I believe your experiences will be delightfully rewarding.

—Evelyn C. Rysdyk

Acknowledgments

If we are lucky, we have people in our lives who lovingly encourage us to give our very best efforts. I have been blessed with many. Each of you, in your own unique and wonderful way, has helped this book come to fruition.

To my family and my friends, I offer my profound thanks for their ongoing support of my growth, creative expression and spiritual expansion. To my teachers in ordinary reality, I offer thanks for their gifts and guidance. To my unseen teachers, I honor your loving ability to continue encouraging me through my resistance.

Thanks also to Samuel Weiser, Inc. It has been a special delight to have this book published in my adopted home of Maine.

MODERN SHAMANIC LIVING

1

Claiming Our Inheritance

Somehow, as a society, we have misplaced our vibrancy and forgotten our true nature. Many people in our world suffer from doubt, depression, insecurity, anxiety, and deep sadness. It is clear that, if the widespread use of antidepressants is any indication, we are witnessing a massive cultural epidemic of joyless living. We feel isolated and alone, having lost contact with our wondrous and magical selves. Yet, even within this devastating emotional maelstrom there is a glimmer of hope. There are still beings who retain the title to joy.

Stored inside the spiral stairway of our genetic material is all our human history. Every evolutionary pirouette we have ever danced as a species is encoded in the twists of our DNA ladder. In the language of amino acids, we remember the upright leap of *Australopithecus* onto the African plain, *Homo erectus's* graceful wandering across the continents, *Homo sapien's* arrival, the great Ice Ages, and all the reaching and reasoning that has brought us here to the close of the 20th century. And, it is in this amazing genetic library that we begin the search for who we are to become in the next millennium.

2 Modern Shamanic Living

Anthropologist Jeremy Narby theorizes that DNA, the foundation of our genetic code, functions as the *axis mundi*—the central core of creation—which is the Universal Intelligence and source of all knowledge. He further proposes that while in a shamanic trance/journey state it is possible to access this source.

Narby believes that shamanic visions may actually be generated by the DNA that is inside and all around us—in plants, animals, birds, and insects—and that through shamanic journey imagery we are able to communicate with the inter-linked biosphere. He supports this proposal by comparing the visions of a shamanic trance/journey, which are often brilliant, glowing, and involve holographic depth, with the images mechanically produced by a coherent light source or laser. Studies in the 1980s determined that all DNA emits photons in the relatively narrow wavelength band of visible light (900–200 nanometers) and while weak, also exhibits laserlike coherency.[1] Therefore, when we choose to enter into this "library of life" through the shamanic journey, we have access to the wisdom of all creation and time periods that would, under ordinary circumstances, be invisible. This invisible world is what tribal shamans refer to as the world of the spirit.

Amid all the shadows of who we once were, there are those wishing to share their insights with us. Both restless and patient, they wait at the edge of our conscious minds. We have not subjugated them with our civilization. They are still sniffing the breeze

---

[1] Jeremy Narby, *The Cosmic Serpent* (New York: Penguin/Putnam, 1998), pp. 125–131.

and watching the horizon. They are still listening to thunder and searching the hillsides. They are alive. They are inside. They are the hunters and gatherers. These ancient human selves understand the delicate balance of all life, the nuances of nature, and the experience of being completely embodied—in the moment. They understand that they hold no dominion over Earth and her creatures. Instead, they see themselves as lovingly interwoven into the fabric of life, holding no illusions of separateness. They must stay in touch with weather and wind—knowing the signs, trusting the signals. They follow the subtle traces the game animals leave as markers in their passing. They sustain themselves, tied to the seasons of each plant's ripening. They see their lives, not as a series of steps to a goal, but as a process that is endless and flowing. There are no guarantees of prizes at the end of the trail; there is only the magic of the path itself.

This way of thinking seems remarkably contrary to the manner in which our society perceives the world. In fact, in a 1987 article in *Discover Magazine,* physiologist Jarad Diamond argues that "Agriculture is the worst mistake in the history of the human race."[2] Studies by paleopathologists have shown clear evidence that ancient hunter/gatherer skeletons indicate that they tended to be stronger and more robust, showing fewer signs of degenerative disease processes than later agricultural societies.[3]

When we stepped out of the hunter/gatherer model of societal organization we began to use our

---

[2] Jared Diamond, "The Worst Mistake in the History of the Human Race," *Discover* (May 1987), p. 64–66.
[3] Diamond, "The Worst Mistake," p. 65.

abilities to change the face of the land and control the fate of other species. No other species on the planet has attempted this control. And this choice has created immense difficulty. In exercising our controls, we have fallen victim to the resulting destruction of our environment. As a society, we have come to believe the illusion that, because we have the ability to shape our environment, we have some sort of superiority over other forms of life. We have forgotten our place in the larger scheme.

Following the same line of hierarchical thinking, our inner environment is dominated by the beliefs and controls of our mind, at the increasing expense of the wisdom of our bodies and our spirits.

We have created a stratified model for our entire existence. Our days, weeks, and years are relentlessly scheduled to include everything we *must* do. Our inattention to the growing compartmentalization of our inner and outer worlds has led us to stumble into a snare that is tightening around us. Like an industry that is single-mindedly in search of more efficient production, we are losing much of what we once held precious. This model is smothering our creativity and our humanity, and extinguishing our joy. We struggle fruitlessly against the bonds, even tricking ourselves into believing that, by scheduling leisure activities and dedicating time to spiritual pursuits, we will be released. Yet, it is becoming clear that, as long as this compartmentalized paradigm is allowed to persist, especially *inside* ourselves, we will not experience the true breadth of our capacity for joyful living.

This painful revelation may lead some of us to feelings of anger, despair, and even terror—making the noose seem tighter still. We wonder how this tragic situation can be changed and how we can find our way back to joy.

Fellow traveler, take heart. I profoundly believe that the sacred ways of health and balance may be restored to us and to Earth. It isn't too late. Since we have done all we can do, as civilized humans, to change the world, the time has come to surrender and to allow the inner hunter to lead us. The hunter/gatherer has never forgotten the way. This compassionate teacher can show us the path to freedom and a richer existence.

The concept of the inner hunter/gatherer may seem irrelevant to us as we witness all that is going on in our personal lives and our culture in this computerized, on-line world. Many of us are already feeling overwhelmed, or even trapped—how could we take in one more piece of information? It is my belief that the very tools we need to make the leap to more vital and healthy living—for ourselves and for the planet—are available through this inner character.

It was once thought that hunting and gathering tasks were carried out by different members of the society. It was believed that the gathering of plants, roots, and berries was usually done by the women in a group or tribe, while hunting was a job for men. More recent studies have shown that Ice Age women in traditional hunter/gatherer bands most likely snared small game and fished with nets in addition to gathering eggs, plants, fruits, and cereal grains.[4] On the other hand, while men most probably gathered some foodstuffs during a hunt for game, it was

---

[4] Heather Pringle, "New Women of the Ice Age," *Discover* (April 1998), p. 67.

not really practical to combine this gathering activity with the rigors of hunting large game, especially while on foot. As we see in contemporary examples, these hunts weren't always successful. So the responsibility to provide what has been estimated as 70 percent of the consumable food fell largely to the women.[5] In fact, without the large quantities of edible plant material gathered by women, along with the small game and fish they hunted, early human beings would have perished. Unlike carnivores, omnivorous humans suffer protein poisoning if fed a diet consisting exclusively of meat.

Whatever the actual breakdown of tasks, the basic skills necessary for both hunting and gathering were clearly very much the same. Searching for game as part of a hunt, or wandering in search of edible and medicinal plants require similar instinctual and behavioral attributes that will become clearer as we examine them.

For the purpose of this book, and in light of recent research, the hunter and gatherer will be merged into a single inner character, the hunter/gatherer. This character is neither exclusively male nor female. Let us discover and examine this inner hunter/ gatherer's attributes from the standpoint of how they can help us in our daily lives.

Our ancestors shared their world with many extraordinary creatures. From the available fossil record and the art that our Ice Age relatives left behind in places like the Chauvet Caves, we know their world was populated by huge and quite fearsome creatures. Our genetic forebearer had to reckon with more than

---

[5] Pringle, "New Women," p. 67.

the easily recognized and famous woolly mammoths. They also lived beside animals as varied as giant bison, rhinolike beasts, cave lions and the cave bear.[6] The cave bears offered a unique danger, as they often lay hidden, hibernating within the exact sort of caves humans often sought out as shelter. To give a clearer perspective, an average North American black bear *(Ursus americanus)* weighs between 200 to 450 pounds.[7] The now-extinct cave bear *(Ursus spelaeus)* weighed about 880 pounds, which is about twice the size of a large black bear.[8] Imagine coming upon one of these with nothing stronger than a stone-tipped wooden spear!

In stark contrast to their fearsome neighbors, humans—relatively small creatures with no claws, poor hearing, limited eyesight, and blunt teeth—had to use tools and skills beyond their simple stone weapons in order to survive. The Paleolithic hunter/gatherer had the very necessary ability to take in the entire landscape. Like a bird at the feeder, who's feeding rhythm is to take only a few pecks and then glance around for the neighbor's cat, we, too, had to remain aware of all of the local creatures' activities. To avoid the very real hazard of being eaten, we had to maintain an expanded perception or awareness.

In fact, referring to the landscape in their terms, we have to include many seemingly divergent elements,

---

[6] Jean-Marie Chauvet, Elliette Brunel Deschamps, and Christian Hillaire, *Dawn of Art: The Chauvet Cave* (New York: Harry N. Abrams, 1996), p. 31.

[7] William H. Burt (Peterson Field Guide #5) *A Field Guide to the Mammals, North America North of Mexico* (Boston and New York: Houghton Mifflin, 1980 edition), p. 45.

[8] Paul Shepherd, *The Sacred Paw: The Bear in Nature, Myth and Literature* (London and New York: Arkana, 1985), p. 3.

including the reactions and movements of game animals, the movements of predators (who could frighten game or jeopardize the hunter himself), the weather conditions (wind can throw an arrow or spear off its mark), the interactions of other beings in the band, and, quite certainly, many more variables. I believe that this ability to hold the larger picture in the present moment's consciousness, while remaining intensely focused on a task (hunting), gave the hunter a unique perspective.

This capacity to perceive, in any moment, the actions and potential reactions inherent in any activity gave the hunter/gatherer the ability to consciously understand interconnectedness. This skill is beneficial because our current cultural inability to act from a deep understanding of these connections can put our lives at risk—not simply our physical existence, but also our ability to have truly joyful emotional lives.

In effect, by compartmentalizing our worldview—that is, by not seeing the whole landscape—we allow ourselves to be *ambushed*, maybe not by a hungry lion or cave bear, but by other distressing scenarios. In failing to observe the complete picture, we fall prey to situations ranging from abusive interactions with other people or systems, to being overwhelmed by our own personal emotional issues, to feeling threatened by Earth's dwindling resources, or even to being victimized by our sociopolitical status (as women, disabled people, single mothers, undocumented aliens, gay people, people of color, etc.). Additionally, this compartmentalized viewpoint can trap us in another illusion—the illusion that whatever we are experiencing in the moment is *all* that is real.

This myopic illusionary focus is what helps to pull us into denial. It is also how we allow our power to be given over to others, and to our systems. We inadvertently hurt ourselves, other people, and the planet in our fear of stepping out of the illusion of our safe compartment.

I've had personal experience of how these habitual cultural compartments can constrain us, even in relatively unthreatening situations. One particular anecdote comes to mind. My partner and I spent time studying with an indigenous shaman. A group had been gathered together to share the wisdom of this highly respected, elderly man, who was a shaman of his people.

The weather was unbearably hot, with the thermometer bubbling over 100°F the entire week. One afternoon, I found myself sitting under a tree with this teacher. The people who functioned as his translators had, for some reason, left him alone. He was sitting, softly singing and talking to the plants. My heart filled so much upon seeing him. I wanted to sit with him. Through gestures, I was able to communicate my wish. He smiled and nodded, and so I kept him company. I could not understand his language; nevertheless, he spoke to me, gesturing to trees and birds. Some other people gathered at the periphery. Through his gestures, we could feel at least some of what he wanted to share with us.

After an hour or so, as I sat at his side, I could see that the teacher was beginning to suffer from the high temperature. His heritage had given him a lessened ability to tolerate heat. I felt myself getting worried and agitated. I perceived that he was in trouble; but I also felt some fear about offending him or perhaps being wrong about what I had perceived. All these conflicting thoughts rapidly flashed through my mind. The others who had gathered were nervous as well, but they also weren't taking any action.

If I stepped out of my "box" and was wrong, there could be consequences. I could offend this elder, look foolish in front of others, and possibly ruin my entire week. In the very instant I had that thought, something occurred that suddenly enabled me to see the entire landscape.

This man had been presented to us as a wise and ancient teacher, existing on a different spiritual level than the rest of us. Yet, clearly, in that moment, he was also a gentle, old man getting overheated! Something inside of me—that which perceived the situation from a new vantage point—*impelled* me to take the risk. I rose, fetched a tiny bit of ice and a wet cloth and came back to his side. Through gestures I asked to place the cloth on his neck. He sighed with relief. I wet his face and his exposed skin with the ice-filled cloth and blew across it to cool him. His quick recovery let me know that I'd made the right call.

I wondered about that incident for months. What had made it possible for me to transcend my perceived limitations in that situation? Somehow, I had unconsciously tapped into a different perspective. If it was there, inside of *me*, it was probably inherent in *every* human being. The challenge was to find out what mechanism within me produced this outcome.

Using a combination of shamanic journey work and my dreams, I began to get a sense of where inside of me this altered perspective on the world was kept. Through my explorations I became aware of this inner character—the hunter/gatherer.

We have, over time, evolved our understanding of the world so that we believe that, by staying within the boundaries of our little world, if we tow the line, we will be kept safe. However, increasingly we see that this is simply not true. The larger landscape always intrudes. We find ourselves struggling to have relationships that are rewarding. We find our job security suddenly slipping through our fingers. We fall into despair and seek to salve our wounds with alcohol, or food, or other distractions. Yet we stubbornly, and perhaps fearfully, cling to the illusion. A part of us knows that this complacency is not contentment, for we need the hunter/gatherer's wise guidance to shift toward a more meaningful, joyful, and fulfilling life.

It is important to remember that the entire landscape of creation is connected. As each one of us claims our inner hunter/gatherer's gifts, we change the whole playing field.

2

Weaving the Path

Another of the hunter's skills that we could certainly use is the process model of knowing the world. Reclaiming a belief in process is, in fact, the single most important tool we have for getting ourselves unstuck.

It is paramount to remember that we already know something of the hunter/gatherer. While the hunter remains an *unconscious* participant in our lives, this part of ourselves can only exert within us a longing and restlessness. Many of us channel our restless energy into career ambition. Some of us use this energy to create trauma in our lives—that horrendous "making a mountain out of a mole hill" syndrome! In our goal-centered paradigm, the gifts of the gatherer are interpreted by us as the feeling that, no matter how much we do, we still need to do more. This energy is channeled into searching out and then gathering *things*. Whether they are antiques, baseball cards, CDs, books, or cash, we reach for them in the relentless pursuit of contentment—to little avail.

The hunter may provide the answer to why these actions are not fulfilling. As I suggested earlier, the hunter's skills do not mesh well with the artificially compartmentalized world we have created. They aren't suited for the goal-driven conceptual model we find ourselves living in today.

Our goal-centered outlook on life seems to have developed with the onset of agriculture. At this same time, I imagine, the beginnings of our compartmentalization occurred as well. Agriculture presented a situation in which it became necessary to judge the fertile "goodness" of a particular piece of land. And, since no one wanted to get stuck with "bad" land, we began dividing the land into parcels—"That's yours and this is mine." It seems as if, while we were at it, we continued dividing other things—*my* country, *your* family, *her* religion, or *his* species. These compartments that we created became the way in which we ordered and controlled the world. The squares of the Earth that were now ours to control needed to be tilled, protected, fenced, and, when necessary, subjugated. If a place we wanted was dry, we *fixed* it by pulling water deep out of the Earth. In fact, our industrial society is simply an outgrowth of an attitudinal shift that occurred when we first strove to make the land, the animals, the plants, and other people follow *our* will. A look around reveals that we've been *fixing* the planet and everything else we have touched for millennia.

This "fixing" may also be seen as creating things that are *fixed*—that is, immobile. I feel that, in our desire to control our world, we have created a social and personal model that is confining in its rigid adherence to the focus on the ends at the expense of the means.

If we play out the current goal-centered model to its extreme and dreary finale, we find that our entire human existence is a rush headlong unto death—the ultimate completion. In other words, by our continued focusing on goals, we are missing out on the actual living of our lives.

As we make the shift out of goal-centeredness, we are able to put every part of our life into a new context. We become, in that one shift, less at the mercy of any situation. Here, I mean more than the simple maxim, "This too shall pass." Rather, I refer to a deep understanding that we are always in the *middle of our process.* From the middle, we are able to view only a small portion of the interconnectedness of our existance. This vantage point makes predicting the outcome of complex situations very risky. Yet we find ourselves culturally programed to fix a final resolution to all of our efforts. No wonder we feel stressed!

We would do well to examine the archaic hunter/gatherer lifestyle and begin to recall our common roots in the process. A pivotal fact is that hunting or gathering is never completed in the same way that an entire year's agricultural season closes with a large harvest. The food sources of the hunter/gatherer must be collected continually. *The work is never finished.* This need to continually pursue nourishment provides a unique perspective. It is a paradigm imbued with endless movement, choice, and change. This is the very essence of the process paradigm.

In addition, since the work of survival is never completed, *work* itself becomes integrated into all phases of the lifestyle. Work and play become intertwined. In cultures that still pursue this way of life, joyful songs, games, and children's play all reflect the work of getting food. All the seemingly disparate components of living become inseparable from each other. They are transformed into intricate and endless threads constantly being woven into a fabric that flows out from the great loom of process.

When we recognize that we are always in the middle, we become free to experiment with the colors and patterns, to adjust our thinking and to seek more information, essentially enjoying every single moment. In essence, when we move away from clinging to any one final product, we give ourselves permission to enjoy all the little "products" along the path. Imagine actually loving your job, being in a wonderfully growing relationship, and having a dynamic passion for every phase of your life.

This magical paradigm is what the inner hunter/ gatherer has fiercely protected for many centuries. This part of ourselves is amazingly deft in the ability to maintain the big picture, while remaining faithful to the elements of process.

It is time to reclaim our inner hunter. By making a conscious choice to listen, we can relearn the gifts that the hunter has kept safe for us. In this listening, both men and women can gain a powerful ally capable of rescuing us from the demanding effects of our civilization.

The space outside of what we know is where we will meet this inner ally. We are fortunate to have many techniques available to us for entering the worlds outside of our conscious understanding. In preparation for this great adventure, we'll first explore a meditation that is especially useful in assisting our full consciousness to be receptive, expanded, and grounded.

The Grounded/Expanded Self (A Meditation)

This meditation is very simple to learn and easy to practice in any situation where we need to feel focused, calm, and present. I find that it is an excellent way to begin each day.

Begin by finding a quiet space where you will not be disturbed. Sit down in a comfortable chair that allows your back to be straight, with your feet on the floor.

With your hands folded gently in your lap, close your eyes and take a few moments to breathe. Allow your breaths to be both quiet and full—somewhat like the breaths of the deep sleep state.

As you begin to relax more fully, notice that your breath originates in the center of your chest. Imagine a light there that grows brighter with each breath you take.

As this light grows brighter, see it also expanding to fill your entire chest—and still it is growing brighter.

While continuing to breathe, notice that the light is growing beyond the limits of your chest and beginning to fill your whole torso.

The light, growing ever brighter and expanding, now moves into your arms and legs and into your head as it continues growing more brilliant with each breath.

Your entire body is now filled with light. As you continue to breathe, see that the light has now begun to glow through your skin. It is no longer contained by your body and is growing still brighter.

Allow this radiance to continue expanding, until it extends three feet all around you. The light that is both inside and all around your body even goes down into the floor.

Continue to expand this light even further until its edges reach the outside of the building in which you are sitting.

Notice that the edges of the light are like the surface of your skin. Feel the air moving outside. Notice the temperature. Can you feel the warmth of the Sun or the moonlight? Feel how your lower edge extends deeply into the Earth. Notice textures. Are there other beings inside of your form? Are there trees, plants, or animals playing inside of your light?

Your entire being is full, rich, radiant, beautiful, and divine. Your spirit—your light—completely surrounds your body. This is your true state of being.

You are completely at peace.

When you feel full of this experience, begin to return your light slowly inward, toward your body. None of its wonderful brilliance is lost as it returns.

When the light that is you is again about three feet all around and below and above you, clasp your folded hands tightly together. As you are doing this, recall the sensations of being expanded, grounded into the Earth, completely filled with dazzling light.

Whenever you wish, you will be able to attain this grounded/expanded state by repeating this symbolic gesture with your hands.

Now, gently release your hands and allow the light to return to a distance just beyond your skin. It retains all of its brilliance.

Slowly return your attention to the room in which you are sitting. Take a full, deep, sighing breath and gently open your eyes.

When you feel ready, you may wish to make notes about what you experienced while doing this meditation. Take time to record all that you felt, saw, and heard. In your journal, articulate, as best as you can, the bodily, emotional, and spiritual sensations of being simultaneously grounded and expanded.

Through working with many people, I have found that this state is most useful in assisting them to more easily internalize new information. In addition, this state allows you to feel more centered and present in daily life.

3

Seeking the Hunter

THERE ARE MANY WAYS to connect with your inner hunter. One technique I've used for synchronizing with my ancient self is to eat *wild* foods intentionally. If you decide to explore the wild foods from your area, it's important to explore this idea carefully. If you live near a cranberry bog, you can find ways to pick some cranberries on your own. However, if you don't know anything about mushrooms, it is not wise to try a few forest mushrooms without supervision. Check out the excellent resources provided by local Cooperative Extension services, health food stores, and libraries for information about your regional favorites. Find out what the original, indigenous inhabitants of your area seasonally gathered or hunted. Ask organic farmers about locally made honey or sources of edible flowers. If you are living in a coastal region, find out about wild, gathered sea vegetables. While wild-food sources can include meat, eating wild food to connect with the inner hunter doesn't have to mean hunting animals. Instead, you can eat what some of the local animals eat.

A dominant hunter animal in my state is the black bear. The bear, like the human being, is an omnivore. That is, the bear eats both plants and animals as they are available seasonally. So, in modeling the bear's habits, as early humans may have done, I look for wild foods that are in season.

For instance, every spring in Maine, it is possible to gather and eat wonderful early greens like dandelions or fiddlehead ferns. After a long New England winter, it feels especially nourishing and rejuvenating to eat fresh greens! (I always think of those sleepy bears using tender new shoots to wake up their bodies after a long winter's rest!)

Later in the year, berries ripen on the barrens and mussels can be gathered from the rocky coast. These are some of the foods on which the early people of this region depended for survival. While survival is no longer an issue for most of us, sampling the wild fare of the place where you live can help you to thrive.

Finding out about and eating wild foods gives us an additional benefit. When we develop an appreciation of how the natural world may sustain us, we can more readily allow ourselves to be weaned from the more artificial world. The Earth and her creatures regain their place as our concrete allies. As we are able to relate to the world in this manner, we are in some real sense set free from our artificially contrived boundaries.

To make your experiments worth while, you may want to record them. The following list will help you remember what you explore.

1. *Ask yourself at what times of the year you are most at the mercy of the hunter's restlessness. Are you, for instance, more restless in springtime or in the fall?*

2. *Find out what the native people of your region lived on during each season.*

3. *Channel periods of restlessness into hunting down this information or actually gathering the foods themselves.*

4. *Ask yourself which of your natural instincts may be attributed to your inner hunter. Think about some of your senses or abilities.*

5. *Keep a record of what you realize about your own process.*

Ancient Spirits

Another method available to us for reclaiming our ancient, hunter selves, is the shamanic journey. The shamanic journey process provides us with a doorway to the invisible world, the world of spirit beyond our knowing. The aboriginal peoples of Australia refer to this world as the Dreamtime, as that which exists outside of our understanding of time and space. The word "spirit" comes down to us from the Latin root *spirare*, meaning "to breathe."[1] When embarking on explorations into these invisible worlds, it is useful to remind our anxious minds that this is really just as easy as breathing. It is also poetically appropriate that this spiritual method historically practiced by hunter/gatherer peoples around the globe,[2] be used to reach our own hunter/gatherer.

In some cultures, the shamanic trance was induced at first through the use of psychotropic substances.

---

[1] *American Heritage Dictionary* (Boston: Houghton Mifflin Co., 1982), p. 1179.
[2] Joan Halifax, *Shaman: The Wounded Healer* (London & New York: Thames & Hudson, 1982), p. 5.

Since there were many mind-altering substances available, it was necessary to evolve an extensive shamanic pharmacology. Each substance provided a different experience. One had to understand the spiritual attributes of each, as well as recognize the substances in nature. For instance, Carlos Castaneda's teacher, Don Juan, taught him that *datura inoxia* was violent, possessive, and unpredictable, whereas, *psilocybe mexicana*, was dispassionate and gentle.[3]

Various animal substances may have been utilized as well. We are also beginning to uncover the psychoactive properties that are available in the flesh of some venomous animals. Anthropologist Bethe Hagens suggests that these animal brains may have been used for such shamanic purposes by Cro-Magnon man and argues that this new theoretical approach may affect current interpretations of Paleolithic artifacts.[4]

Along with the use of these many psychoactive substances, many cultures utilized some form of repetitive sound. Ethnographers note the use of drumming by the shamans (or *noides*) as well as the use of the fungus, *amanita muscaria,* in their studies of the Saami people of arctic Europe.[5] In fact, the drum is a tool common to many different shamanic cultures. Although trances were sometimes induced through magical plants, drumming may have been used to sustain the long periods of trance needed by many

---

[3]   Carlos Castaneda, *The Teachings of Don Juan: A Yaqui Way of Knowledge* (New York: Washington Square Press, 1968), pp. 200–230.

[4]   Bethe Hagens, "Venuses, Turtles, and Other Handheld Cosmic Models," in Myrdene Anderson, ed., *On Semiotic Modeling* (Berlin & New York: Mouton de Gruyter, 1991).

[5]   Halifax, *Shaman: The Wounded Healer,* p. 56.

tribal shamans to perform their work. In most cases, drumming alone is effective for inducing an altered or shamanic state of consciousness. Repetitive auditory stimuli have the ability to create vivid visionary states that rival those experienced under the influence of sacred, hallucinogenic botanicals.

The contemporary Western resurgence of shamanism and shamanic techniques was precipitated, in part, by Dr. Michael Harner. In his studies, Harner rediscovered the essential elements necessary to shift humans into the shamanic state. Entering this altered state of consciousness makes transcending barriers of the known world possible.

After extensive exploration of the ecstatic trance of shamans in traditional cultures as diverse as the Jivaro and Conibo of South America, Siberian nomadic groups, the Lakota, and the !Kung of the Kalahari, Harner confirmed that shamans of different regions and cultures, separated by thousands of miles, on separate continents, had remarkably similar experiences.[6] Not only did they seem to travel to spirit regions that were similar, they used related techniques to reach those regions—including the shaman's journey. The shamanic practice that Harner refers to as "core shamanism" contains this experiential thread that is common to all.

The shamanic-journey process, as distilled by Harner, has been taught worldwide under the auspices of his Foundation for Shamanic Studies. Many thousands of people, from widely varied walks of life, from small towns, villages, and urban centers, have

---

[6] Michael Harner, *The Way of the Shaman* (New York: Harper & Row, 1990), pp. 24–25.

found themselves able to participate in these remarkable, ecstatic experiences previously thought to be limited to traditional tribal shamans.

On an expedition by the Foundation for Shamanic Studies to the remote Central Asian Republic of Tuva in 1993, the efficacy of core shamanic practice was put to the test. Western practitioners found themselves reteaching Tuvan shamans the journey practices that were nearly eradicated during the shaman purges of the old Soviet regime.[7] Furthermore, the members of the expedition found that they indeed had a kind of "shamanic language" that they shared with these people. This suggests that each of us has the inherent capacity to embark on a shamanic journey and enter this invisible world. We only need a bit of reminding.

To begin any exploration of shamanism or the journey process, it is imperative that you understand that, in the world of the shaman, *every thing* is living.[8] This spiritual worldview is referred to as *animism*. The spirits of animals, plants, stones, rivers, seasons, winds, and mountains are as palpably real as anything we can touch. The altered state of consciousness that you enter on a shamanic journey, allows you to visit with these extraordinary beings. You are, in this state, able to go *beyond the veil,* and, when you have completed your task, to return safely to this reality.

Shamanic practitioners visit with the spirits for advice, knowledge of hidden information, and heal-

---

[7] Address by Tuvan shaman, Mongush Kenin-Lopsan, at the First Congress of the World Council for Psychotherapy, Vienna, Austria, July 1996.

[8] Halifax, *Shaman: The Wounded Healer*, p. 9.

ing. Whatever the interaction, they always remain humble in the face of the spirits' awesome power. The spirits of the natural world are treated as treasured friends and great teachers.[9] Shamans may seek to communicate with these spirits and perhaps negotiate with them as well, but they do not believe it is possible to become superior to nature. In this framework of belief, it is therefore understandable that shamans often honor these spirits in very concrete ways. The spirits may be honored with ceremonies, dances, songs, prayers, and offerings. Whatever the manifestation, however, these offerings are always expressions of a profound and loving respect.[10]

In fact, many cultures have mythic tales of those who tried to hold dominion over the spirits and failed. These tales have been passed down to remind us of where we fit in the plan—with the deer, the leaf, and the river.

The shamanic hunter/gatherer worldview requires that we give thanks to everything around us. Gratitude becomes a ritualized and living constant in our lives. Since every thing in a process paradigm is living and no thing is static, *nothing* may be taken for granted.

Surely, even ancient Europeans envisioned the world in this reverential manner. In Scandinavia's high arctic, the Saami retained much of their old shamanic past into the last century.[11] Their shaman's drums are decorated with images that honor the spirits and map the invisible, magical realms. These images share an

---

[9] Halifax, *Shaman: The Wounded Healer*, p. 11.

[10] Halifax, *Shaman: The Wounded Healer*, p. 67.

[11] Halifax, *Shaman: The Wounded Healer*, pp. 56–57.

uncanny resemblance to petroglyphs found on Norway's Sørøya Island that have been estimated at 6,000 to 8,000 years old.[12] One has only to observe these carvings or the powerful images that Paleolithic painters left deep in the Earth on the walls of Lascaux and Chauvet to un- derstand, on an emotional and spiritual level, that our European ancestors shared the hunter/gatherer's animist worldview found everywhere on the globe.

As each of us carries the ancestral hunter in our DNA, so too we hold the gatherer's precious perception of the Earth in our genes. The shamanic journey and the shaman's respectful way of interacting with the natural world may revive this original vision of the world in us.

It may be useful to ask yourself the following questions when you explore thinking about your past.

1. *Ask yourself how you relate in general to the world around you.*

2. *Determine which creatures, plants, or places have particular significance to you.*

3. *What part of the natural world gives you the most joy? What frightens you most about the natural world? What excites you in the natural world?*

4. *Question whether seasonal changes affect the way you perceive the world around you.*

---

[12] "Geographica" page, *National Geographic* (October 1993).

4

Preparing to Journey

To begin understanding the shamanic journey process, we must find out what part(s) of ourselves actually travel. To the traditional shaman, the spirit of an individual is capable of taking flight—that is, the spirit may partially leave the body.[1] We are perhaps more comfortable, as Westerners, calling this journeying part of ourselves the consciousness.

The leaving and returning of the spirit/consciousness is done intentionally by the shaman for the purpose of looking outside of ordinary time/space reality. These shamanic journeys were usually undertaken for important reasons. For instance, to a hunter/gatherer group, finding the exact location of a herd of game animals would mean the group's ultimate survival. Animals like caribou have remarkably wide ranges. How could the hunters know when the herd would return and, more importantly, *where* the herd could be found at any given time? Since tracking and hunting, in most instances, were done on foot, even narrowing the focus of the hunt would be extraordinarily beneficial. It was the shaman's job to

---

[1] Piers Vitebsky, *The Shaman* (Boston: Little Brown, 1995), p. 14.

discover this hidden information and then return to his or her people and impart the spirit-given wisdom that was gained on the spirit journey.

Realize therefore, that the journey is incomplete without the return to ordinary reality. The tribe does not benefit if the shaman does not return. In fact, to remain in the world of spirit does not benefit anyone. Even the shaman is jeopardized. In the shamanic view, when the spirit does not fully return to the body, it causes illness and, if the entire soul is lost, even death. The people who go into the Otherworld and do not return, whose psyches remain dislocated, risk both physical and mental illness. What separates the madman from the shaman, therefore, is *intentionality*.[2] Our intentionality begins with a clear understanding of all the steps of the journey process before we undertake our first experience. So our first step toward a safe practice is: *It isn't how far you go, it's how fully you return.*

While shamanic techniques are relatively simple and their results almost immediate, the evolution that an individual undergoes in learning the process is profound and ongoing. As we gain spiritual insight and experience growth, we also sacrifice illusory control. The more we learn about the nature of reality, the more our mind's knowledge seems insignificant. As our heart's understandings gain deeper relevance, we begin a shift from an ego-dominated viewpoint to a spirit/heart dominated perspective.

Castaneda's Yaqui shaman, Don Juan, refers to Paths of the Heart. These heart-centered paths draw the most from life and therefore from the travelers as

---

2 Michael Harner, *The Way of the Shaman* (New York: HarperCollins, 1980), p. 53.

well.[3] But how can we discover the direction of these paths? We can begin by looking at the world through fresh eyes.

When we communicate, in a journey, with a tree, for instance, we can no longer objectify that tree. It is no longer just some *thing* we pass on our travels. It becomes, instead, a fellow traveler accompanying us on our adventure. We, in essence, shift our abstract idea of trees toward a relationship with individual trees. We recognize that, not only is everything living, but each living being has a consciousness. Through the journey, we are able to communicate with these other sentient beings and our world suddenly becomes populated with many more companions. This powerful perceptual shift is necessary to reclaim our inner hunter/gatherers.

So, how do we make journeys? As with ordinary travels, journeys must have a starting place. Each of us has found ourselves, at one time or another, in a place in Nature that we felt was magical or special. It may have been at the ocean, in a meadow, on a hilltop, in a quiet wood, or perhaps a moment from a childhood holiday. In that special place, we may have found ourselves feeling particularly safe or filled with joy, or we may have lost all track of time's passing. This is the place where we will initiate our search for entrances to the shaman's reality—to what Castaneda termed "non-ordinary reality." It doesn't matter if your place no longer exists in this reality. We won't be limited by linear, human history. We will be going outside of our time and space.

<hr>

[3] Carlos Castaneda, *The Teachings of Don Juan: A Yaqui Way of Knowledge* (New York: Washington Square Press, 1968), p. 11.

To search for your entrance to non-ordinary reality, begin by finding, in this reality, a quiet time and comfortable position. Take your phone off the hook, put a "Do not disturb" message on the door, and shut off all your beeping and ringing gadgets! For this process to be successful, you must go off line! You may sit in a favorite chair or lie on the floor. The important thing is to allow your body to fully relax. Close your eyes and take a few minutes to breathe deeply and quietly. Assume the meditative, grounded/expanded state. (Review the meditation in chapter 2, page 17.) Once you have expanded your light, allow your consciousness to return to the most magical of your place memories.

Recall as much information about your special place as you can. Engage all of your sensory input. What time of day is it? Where is the Sun or Moon? Is there a breeze or is it still? Are there scents of flowers, the ocean, pine trees? What is the ground around you like? Be as fully present in this place as you are able and continue to explore. Get to know the trees, plants, and stones of your power-filled place. At some point, you may feel the presence of a friendly animal or bird. Greet this new friend.

When you are quite full with this experience, gently return to the room in which you are sitting or lying. Thank any creatures you met. Take time to breathe deeply once again and, when you feel ready, open your eyes. As soon as possible, record your experience in a journal with as much detail as you are able. These experiences are sometimes as elusive as dreams and recording them—committing them to concrete memory—will assist you in returning to what we will refer to as your *power place*. This is where you will find your entrances to the realms of spirit.

Path of the Bear (A Shamanic Journey Dream Story)

The Southern sky, visible from my bed, is beginning to shade to lavender. What's left of the Sun is striking the tops of the tallest fir trees, revealing their cone-heavy branches. Almost as soon as I notice this, the light changes and the fir cones shrug back into the shadows. As the twilight grows, the trees, clearly individuals in the daytime, merge into a hunkering mass. In the fading light, they gather together and wait.

Just before night, there comes a moment when the silence and stillness are electrifying. The birds seem magically to hush their songs in unison, while disappearing into the blackening forest. This is the bat's time. Like shift workers in a busy plant, they come in to take the place of the swallows, sweeping the sky of creatures that batter the window screens.

The first of the evening stars shimmer to life and find their constellations cut into new patterns by the jagged line of trees. If it were winter, I might catch Orion hunting outside my window. But, recognized or not, my star visitors are welcome, as nights this clear are rare in June.

The starry night fills my mind, tickling a memory. I am standing in a great bowl of trees framing the summer sky all around. This valley is sibling to so many others. People named them to ease their discomfort with the number. This is the one my Dutch ancestors called Pantherkil, the valley of panthers. Tonight there are no big cats padding to the stream. Felines have been replaced by other soft ursine paws. Walking quietly to drink the water that reflects the sky full of stars, the black bears have returned to the valley.

They seem to go together—bears and stars. Some peoples believe that bears came down to Earth from the heavens. The Ostyaks of Siberia say that bears are born of the Sun, Moon, and the Great Bear in the sky. The Little Bear, they say, looked down on the Earth and loved it so much he longed to be here. He went to the Great Bear to ask permission. The Great Bear granted the Little Bear's wish, but gave him strict instructions about how to behave. "Leave the good people alone," Great Bear told him. "Oppress the bad and teach the people the Great Bear Ceremony."

Many peoples who shared the land with bears have such ceremonies. In Europe, Asia, and North America, people tell myths and stories about them still. Our children find comfort in them and even the tamest teddy still holds kinship with his living brethren. These traditions and old truths have a way of lurking in the shadows. The lost stories, songs, and rituals affect us, even when we have no conscious cultural memories of them. Like treasures hidden away, they wait patiently for us to stumble over them and claim them as our own. For me, at least, they seem to speak to some ancient self.

As I drift off to sleep and dream, She springs immediately to life. In my dream, I see a very old woman bent over a shank of bone that she has braced on her fur-robed lap. She is scratching the seasons' passing, the Moon's phases, and the times of bounty on the bone's surface in complex rhythms, as she has done forever. As I approach her, she looks up and holds the bone out for me to see across the aeons. The old woman has so deftly recorded the whorls of life's cycles and the many sacred patterns that I am able to understand them as I would a map.

As I am drawn closer, I realize that she is the dreamer and I am the dreamed! She has created my body out of her songs and bone dust!

When I reach her side, she stands—many-times-great grandmother in shaggy hides littered with the remains of her labors. She turns and beckons me to follow her. As I tag along behind her, tracing the patterns she has laid before me, I see her true self revealed in her footprints—Bear Mother. She leads me, as her kind has always done. She has dreamed us into being while sleeping in her den. She has taught us what is safe to eat and where the sweetest waters flow. We have sought shelter in her caves. She has guided our steps around the Earth, who's seasons conduct themselves along the courses she has charted. Stasis has no place here. In this world, all is in endless, vibrating motion.

Ahead of me, I see her slowly waving her paws in circles: "Life. Death. Rebirth." She huffs and the air fills with strangely arousing scents of earth, blood, musk, and honey. The trees grow green, turn amber, loose their leaves and resprout in a dizzying succession. Hypnotic rhythms pass into and around each other with her every lumbering footfall. Tumbling like pebbles in a brook, wandering with the wind, my pulse surges in my ears. I am throbbing with life.

She growls to me softly: "Follow the Path . . ."

". . . of the Bear," I whisper in reply, and the constellations wheel rapidly overhead as we, mother and
cub, disappear into the darkness.

5

Guide to the Realms

THE SHAMAN'S WORLD of spirit is often seen as divided into three distinct regions: the Middleworld, the Upperworld, and the Lowerworld. For the purposes of working safely with our hunter/gatherer, we will be journeying to the latter two. These two realms are the safest for journeys of healing, information, and power. The spirits in these two realms, the Upperworld and Lowerworld, are wise beings or higher spirits that are willing to assist us in our lives.

The Middleworld is where we all live, but outside of the current time/space. In the Middleworld are found the spirits of those who are living now, as well as those spirits that have remained here after the passing of their bodies. Although there are many powerful, gentle, and helpful spirits in Middleworld, there are also spirits that behave in negative ways. Some human spirits in the Middleworld haven't "moved into the light." As a result, these spirits may retain those petty human traits of trickery, jealousy, greed, hatred, or may exhibit great cruelty. In fact, the spirits of the dead can become troublesome to the living—being destructive, stealing souls, disturbing dreams, or being otherwise disprutive. In other words, they're simply not the sort of beings on whom you would rely for solid advice! Recognizing this, we'll make our connections to the spirits that are accessed through the Lowerworld and the Upperworld. For the work of this book, we'll rely on these more trustworthy spirits.

Let us begin with the Lowerworld. This place in non-ordinary reality has parallels in nearly every culture. Whether you name it Alice's Wonderland or the realm of the "fair folk," it is usually an incredibly vivid, vibrant, and power-filled place.

Most often it is described as resembling the primordial, pristine Earth, with all of her biozones in splendid, living profusion. You may find brilliant deserts, green valleys, flowery meadows, snow-capped mountains, great oceans, rivers with mighty waterfalls, and steaming jungles. All of these places in the Lowerworld are filled with spirits, but not only those of animals and plants as you might expect!

In this remarkable place, the spirits of creatures we think of as mythical coexist with the spirits of those found in our current zoological texts. You may find dragons, unicorns, centaurs, giant talking plants, blue oxen, extinct beasts, and other fantastic creatures in the Lowerworld. Here, they are just as real as any other being. Perhaps humans glimpsed these mythical animals in their visits to the Lowerworld and then wove wonderful tales about them. We can never be sure. Just be open to these journey experiences, remembering that what we know about the world and the cosmos may be incomplete. It has certainly happened many times before in our human history that the truth of one age has been supplanted by the truth of the next!

To reach the realm of the Lowerworld, we enter into and pass through the Earth. Entrances to the Lowerworld are as diverse as the journeyers themselves. In teaching many people to journey over the years, my partner and I have seen a tremendous variety of paths. People use animal burrows, openings in hollow trees, caves, deep pools, subway tunnels, coal chutes, manholes, and even closets, as described in the children's storybook *The Lion, the Witch, and the Wardrobe*! Some people may also use different entrances to reach different areas of the Lowerworld.

Whatever the path, the opening always seems to have some magical significance to the journeyer. Quite often they are found in one of the person's power places. These power spots in the Middleworld exist partially outside of our ordinary reality. They are places where the veil between the realms is easily penetrated. These so-called "thin places" seem also to be protected in some way from troublesome Middleworld spirits. We generally feel safe there, even when their energies produce tingles and surges in our bodies! It is my belief that these places are safe zones, created and protected by beneficial Middleworld spirits so that we may reach the Otherworlds.

Entrances in the Middleworld are also used to access the Upperworld. This magical, spirit region is found above the known world and, like the rest of the Otherworlds, outside of this ordinary reality. Since we are the first generation of humans to physically leave the surface of our planet, it may be more difficult to imagine the boundaries of such a place. We have to remember that we are not going into outer space. We are going *outside* of space and time. We are traveling, in our journeys, to the ancient, unlimited worlds of spirit. We are going beyond.

The Upperworld has been described in many ways by many cultures. Even though it is referred to in different cultures by different words, remarkable parallels exist from one culture to another.

The Huichol people of Central Mexico refer to the Upperworld as the "sky world."[1] Siberian shamans refer to the sky people, who may be reached by flying through the Pole Star.[2] The Wiradjuri of Australia ascend to the sky realm, which they refer to as "Baiame's camp." (Baiame is the wise old being whose sons and daughters are the birds and beasts.)[3] The legendary Old Norse land of Valhalla may have evolved from the more ancient shamanic sky world. It is said that only valiant warriors were allowed access to the Great Hall in Valhalla. The greatest of these warriors were said to have been *berserkers* in battle—that is, they wore bearskins and became "like bears."[4] This magical animal transformation has direct roots in shamanic beliefs. In many cultures, powerful shamans often transform themselves into animals or birds to accomplish their shamanic tasks. We will be speaking more about transformation later in the book.

References to the Upperworld, or a world found above the Earth, are also found in fables and children's stories. For instance, we have been told about a boy named Jack who climbed a beanstalk of enor-

---

[1]   Piers Vitebsky, *The Shaman* (Boston: Little Brown, 1995), p. 49.
[2]   Vitebsky, *The Shaman*, p. 101.
[3]   Joan Halifax, *Shamanic Voices* (New York: E. P. Dutton, 1979), p. 54.
[4]   Paul Shepherd, *The Sacred Paw: The Bear in Nature, Myth and Literature* (London & New York: Arkana, 1985), p. 124.

mous proportions and reached a new land. Certainly Dorothy's magical Land of Oz is another example of the Upperworld. She ascended from this world in a tornado, finally landing in a place reached only by going "over the rainbow." This use of rainbow imagery is also found in many cultures. The rainbow is seen by many peoples as a bridge to the Otherworld. In the South Pacific, the mythic Hawaiian hero, Aukelenuiaiko, reaches heaven by way of such a bridge. In ancient Greece, rainbows were the domain of the goddess Iris, who was a messenger between the Earth and sky.[5]

In fact, Dorothy's whirlwind is only one method of reaching the Upperworld. Rising smoke from a campfire may also offer a way to ascend, as can sparks flying up a chimney. The wind may carry the shaman off his special mountain and through a crack in the sky. Likewise, the seeker of the Upperworld may climb a magic plant or a great tree.

In fact, magical, great trees are universal symbols and are commonly used as a way for shamans to travel up or down. This World Tree is often depicted as growing through the worlds, functioning as a support for the heavens and holding the Earth together. An axial pole or pillar of the world is seen, from South America to Siberia, as the bridge between the realms. This World Tree was called Yggdrasil in the old Norse legends. The Sora of India also share this World Tree imagery. Their shamans, who are often women, must climb the tree to reach their helping spirits. To make these climbs easier, the shamans

---

[5] Alexander Eliot, *The Universal Myths* (New York: New American Library [A Meridian Book], 1990), p. 99.

may transform themselves into birds or animals such as the monkey, who is skilled in climbing.[6]

Flying like birds, either up through the branches of the World Tree or through the sky, is also a traditional method for going upward. So, too, is being carried up on the back of a great bird or some other flying beast. A flying horse, such as Pegasus, may be used to leave a high place—a mountaintop—to begin a journey into the Upperworld.

As with your entrance to the Lowerworld, your entrance to the Upperworld will be found in one of your personal power places. Remember, you have this magical understanding of the world in your genetic code. Allow some time to re-imagine yourself in those special places and you will see where you need to go. These are the first steps on the path to reclaiming the gifts of your ancient self.

It bears repeating that the edges of what you can define as reality will be stretched a bit in this reclamation. You may indeed find that what you have believed all your life to be real will be challenged. This is a natural part of spiritual evolution. As stated earlier, those who connect to the spirits of the plants or animals begin to perceive the Earth and her creatures differently. A new level of humility may fill you, bringing with it a growing compassion for all of God's creatures. You may begin to recognize that you are an incredibly tiny piece of creation. You may also simultaneously recognize that you are as divinely beautiful as any other part.

I enjoyed the privilege of experiencing a week-long, intensive training session during the summer

---

6 Vitebsky, *The Shaman*, p. 70.

of 1996 with the late Mikail Duvan, the last male shaman of the Ulchi of Siberia. All during the week, he prayed with the spirits, asking them to look kindly on all who were gathered. He begged the spirits to take pity on us—in spite of our ignorance. This viewpoint included himself and extended to all humans, whatever their station in life.

As he fervently prayed in a ritual, he said to the spirits: "I'm just a little person. I don't know anything." In spite of his long life and what I can only imagine to be a huge accumulation of life experience, he was a deeply humble man.

Perhaps *this* is wisdom—realizing that, the more you learn, the less you actually know! Certainly, this appears to be so in many cultures. It is why we need to retrace our steps along the spiral path, back toward the waiting hunter.

The Doorway (A Shamanic Journey Dream Story)

Standing in a dimly lit room, I am facing a massive doorway. Reaching high above the floor, the top of this entrance curves into an arch with a still-higher arched center. This lends the doorway a roughly human appearance on a gigantic scale.

All around the doorway is a very wide, wood moulding that is carved with rhythmically styled flames and clouds. Raised surfaces of the carving are polychromed in yellows, reds, and blues, interwoven with delicately applied gold leaf in all the recesses. The gold repeats the colors of the paint, and my own reflection, in a warm, visual echo.

As fantastic as it is, this extraordinary frame pales in comparison to the impossible hallucination that is the door. Imagine the Northern Lights seen from all directions at once, miraculously compressed into a flat membrane of light. Marvelous plays of color convulse in a constantly changing flow, freely associating themselves in combinations never before seen by human eyes. Senses are hopelessly seduced by this phenomenal vision. It mesmerizes the body, bringing it closer, and proximity to its mad writhing produces a delicious experience.

Emanating from this light is an extremity of joy that tugs the body into cellular aching. Organs and bones are humming exotic melodies, as tears well up and fall musically to the floor. The whine of neurons, firing all together, exclaim in deafening counterpoint and eyes beam out the light they ordinarily receive. Inner and outer worlds harmonize in an endless, orgasmic crescendo as I step over the threshold.

There are sinuous colors entwining themselves all around my body. Submerged in this auroral fantasy, experiencing exhilaration and claustrophobia simultaneously, my mind is completely overwhelmed. Responding to this magical landscape, my brain can only whimper its objections to the utter lack of landmarks. "No up . . . no down . . . no horizon . . ." it wails, over and over, like a terrified child.

Waves of compassion begin to lap over my fear-stricken mind.

"You are held within me," my voice coos softly from every pore, as my edges expand beyond the limit of my skin. Now my body, too, is cradled in a growing form. This new self extends out in all directions, becoming a radiant, elliptical sphere—an egg holding the yolk of physical form. Slowly quieting its anxiety, my mind—inside my body, inside the egg—begins to accept the safety of its new dwelling.

This container continues its expansion and, in its reaching out, encounters Another.

Startled at first, my eyes strain, begging to see this companion. They are rewarded with a vaguely human shape standing just inside the gateway. This location suggests a sentinel or guardian. Its form shifts and ebbs, threatening at any moment to return into the undulating light that moves all around us. Stretching gently forward, we touch and, amazingly, extend into each other. There is, first, a tingling sensation, then mutual inquiries are exchanged.

"Welcome, Dear One," the being greets me. "For what purpose have you come?"

Somewhere, far away, my mind begins its nervous mantra and I have to expand myself still further to quell its whimpering.

"I'm not sure why I'm here. And where exactly is here, anyway?" I ask in reply.

"This is the Place of Coming into Form."

"What form? Coming in from where?"

"From those dimensions without form," the Guardian counters.

"I don't understand." My mind's nattering has gotten more insistent.

"Your place is one of three-dimensional form, Dear One. It is the only domain that offers this possibility. Beings who wish the opportunity to experience a body enter from this place."

The idea that the body is simply a possibility—one variation among many available to the spirit—is something my mind finds nearly impossible to comprehend.

The human brain has spent countless aeons categorizing and compartmentalizing every experience of the flesh. That is all it knows. No wonder these heretical ideas make it tremble with inconceivable anxiety!

"Why do you want to take form?" I ask.

"We would wish you to ask yourself this question, Dear One."

This circular conversation is starting to perturb my little gray cells.

"Why am I in form? I don't know."

The Guardian begins a vibration that feels, to my beleaguered little mind, a lot like laughter. Insulted, my mind draws itself up to fight but, finding no resistance, it hunkers down. It is confused about how to proceed. Eventually, in spite of itself, curiosity overcomes suspicion and my mind gathers itself to pay attention to the answer. As it settles down, new impressions begin and I am propelled to the beginning place.

Familiar and pleasant memories begin to fill my entire being. There are many others here with me and this is a tender homecoming. We are together in light, everyone floating, moving endlessly, yet also still. The center is everywhere, inside and around. We are one and many. There are no barriers, no need for time, as moments are created from inner urgings. This is how choices are made and possibilities decided among infinite likelihoods.

Some choose that which is unavailable in this place of formless beauty—to enter the dominion of senses and bring this experience back to the whole. However, this taking of physical form is not chosen lightly. To affect physical reality and interact with that dimensional realm is a choice that demands thoughtful consideration, as there is a sacrifice. On the Earth, in a body, it is possible to forget all that is understood here. There is something inherent in the process that interferes with the ability to remember who we are and the true nature of reality. In the for-getting, those in body feel lost and abandoned. For many of us, the realization that there are brothers and sisters who experience this pain of isolation is the impetus to our own embodiment. In the fullness of compassion, we choose to enter—knowing that, in helping others recall their sacred connection, we risk the same loneliness, desperation, and pain.

Compassion and profound desire rise up to out-weigh all cautions. I choose to enter—Form.

Reality twists. Now, inside the illumination, the dark beckons and throbs. There is a flush of excite-ment as something in the darkness draws me closer. It is small and I am rushing toward it. Entering this space nearly devoid of light, panic hits and I scramble to feel my connection. Relieved to realize that I'm still safely tethered to the many, amazing new sensations begin. First, there is sweet sound—a muffled drum-ming. Listening at the edges of that sound, I can hear another, much slower drumming surrounding the first. Pulsating and soothing, the sounds pull more of me into this floating, warm blackness, until, all at once, I am wrenched away—torn free.

One sharp, bright breath and I am pushed into separation. There is scarce time to question or mourn. No time for anguish, as body occupies and engages my entire being. An onslaught of sensory input floods ev-ery receptor. Limbs move with a restless thrashing and lungs expand to draw in the Earth's breath. My eyes squint against this experience of light, so different from the bright place through which I entered this world.

Most of these new experiences are almost painful in their intensity, but there is one that is enormously pleasant. Skin! It is a miraculous new receptor. When I am touched on this envelope about me, I am almost brought back to the place of One. So very comforting in this strange place of edges and boundaries. My body is being lifted up, held, and rocked. The temporary relief from separation quickly soothes my new body to a blissful rest.

In the darkness of sleep, the body loosens its tight grip on the spirit. Once again able to travel freely, the spirit seeks to explore every inch of this new reality. Reaching out to regain what is lost, it flows into each niche, searching out other forms and creating further transformation.

I am transported again!

Waking from the dream, my eyes are smeared with remnants of my nap. The roof of the den is shedding soil on my head as I yawn and roll onto my back. As I stir, the smell of the earth mixes with my own scent and that of the greasy leaves under my haunch.

Scratching at a spot made uncomfortable by a misplaced twig, I realize my belly is empty. So, turning to face the entrance, I squeeze myself out into the early spring dawn. Gingerly testing my legs, I stand for a while, blinking at the glare. My legs feel stiff and heavy as I wobble my way through the wooded hillside and down to the brook. Just as walking is begin-

ning to limber up my body, one leg gives out momen-
tarily and I have to catch myself to keep from falling,
face first, into the water.

As I stand, regaining both balance and dignity, my
belly again reminds me of my purpose. Even though
snow still covers much of the ground, I know food is
here. At my stomach's gnawing insistence, I begin
moving aside leaves, searching for the sprouts that
are just starting their way toward the sunlight. These
tasty treasures, once found, are nibbled slowly to re-
acquaint my body with food. My insides, as well as
my outsides, are stretching, yawning, and grumbling
their way out of sleep with every luscious mouthful.
There are so many different kinds of shoots to be discovered! Some of them are slightly bitter. These are
especially good, as they remind me to drink the
crystal-clear water flowing in the brook. It's all part of
the awakening.

I continue to browse and drink, until the sunlight
pours evenly over the forest floor. Having satisfied my
hunger and feeling the welcome warmth of this mid-
morning Sun on my back, I sleepily settle down on a
broad, flat rock.

Drowsing in the tree-dappled light, I am suddenly
besieged by flying insects. Singing—almost too rapidly to be understood—into my ears, they swarm
around my head. The song is their family's ancestral
saga about the glory of wings. Just this morning,
these innocents have dried their newfound append-
ages into hardness and they finally understand the
ancient lyrics passed to them by their elders. They
have discovered, with giggling delight, that they can
actually use these wondrous gifts to leave the ground!

Their joyous celebration, spot-lit by a sunbeam, is performed as an energetic chorus of buzzing woven through the fragrant air.

Flicking each ear in turn, I chase the tiny choir from side to side, until they finally fly off to proclaim their joy to the rest of the spring forest.

Sighing my way to my feet, I get on with my own part of the celebration. As I wend my way over a ridge, the insect song repeats itself in my mind. The sounds tumble around, weaving themselves into one single note—joy!

6

A Journey to the Lowerworld

Shamans the world over use sounds to help them in their work. Across time and around the globe, drumming is a common method of sustaining the shamanic state of consciousness. Sustaining that state is a necessary component in our being able to depart from our power place.

The kind of drumming that we need to shift our consciousness is a repetitive 205 to 220 beats per minute.[1] This sustains the shamanic state for the duration of the journey. In addition to the repetitive nature of the sound, it has been documented that drum frequencies of 4 to 7 cycles per second, closely replicate EEG-measured theta-wave states that are related to trancelike states of consciousness.[2]

This method of producing the shamanic state is safe and flexible. By using drumming, you may stop the experience whenever you want, instead of waiting for psychotropic chemicals to leave your system. In addition, you are able to hold a clear-minded intent for your experience. This allows you to use the journey

---

[1] Michael Harner, *The Way of the Shaman* (New York: HarperCollins, 1980), p. 31.
[2] Harner, *The Way of the Shaman*, p. 52.

process as a problem-solving and question-asking tool.

You may drum for yourself, have a friend drum for you, or as many people do, use a recording that has been specifically created to sustain the journey state. These tapes and CDs have the added benefit of allowing you to use earphones. When you live in an apartment, this is quite useful! These recordings also have a call-back signal recorded on them. The call-back signal allows you to further relax into the journey process, knowing that you will be called back and will not get lost!

The call-back signal found on most shamanic drumming recordings is four loud groups of seven beats each, followed by a rapid return rhythm lasting approximately 30 to 45 seconds. This is followed by a final series of four units of seven beats. (I've grown so used to hearing this call-back signal that I once used it to get myself back together after being violently startled awake by my alarm clock! I closed my eyes, tapped out the call-back, and felt myself returning gently to this reality, as if from a journey!)

As you did for your power-place exercise, provide yourself with a quiet space where you will be undisturbed. Prepare yourself by entering the grounded/expanded state once again. Set your drumming tape at a comfortable level through the headphones. Even though one side of a drumming tape is typically 20 to 30 minutes long, you may fast-forward it partway to have a shorter initial journey. Get yourself comfortable. Have something handy to cover your eyes. A cloth, blindfold, or sleep mask will work well. With the drumming in your ears and the sights of the ordinary world blocked out, you will be able to more fully enter the experience of non-ordinary reality.

First we will visit the Lowerworld. Since this spirit region is found below this world, we must find our way down.

Start your first Lowerworld journey in your power place. Look around that place for a way to enter into the Earth. You may find a cave, an animal den, a hollow tree, a rabbit hole, or even a man-made doorway. Once you enter this opening, you will *intend* to go down to the Lowerworld. The way down may resemble a tunnel or tube, but it may also be a ramp or some other sort of passageway. For instance, my mother's journeys to the Lowerworld are accomplished entirely on a great staircase. The important thing is that you travel *downward*. (If you travel horizontally, instead of down, you may pop up, scratching your head like Bugs Bunny and wondering about that "wrong turn you took at Albuquerque!") Just repeat your intention, continue to travel down, and don't forget to breathe.

It is important to note at this juncture the extraordinary human gift of active imagination. This is essential to initiating the journey process. This is not cheating and it doesn't mean you'll be "making it all up." Instead, by actively pursuing the journey, you are communicating to the spirits your free choice to enter their realm for guidance. This is a necessary component, since the spirits in the Lowerworld and Upperworld are not allowed to interfere with human free will.

At some point in your journey, you will perceive a shift from your own mind's imagery to the images and actions of the spirits. Be persistent, be patient, and the process will unfold.

When you have entered the Lowerworld, begin to look around. As you did in your power place, take time to engage all of your senses. What sort of environment surrounds your spirit body? Are there animals, birds, and plants nearby?

Look around you for an animal that appears to want to engage with you, or one that seems to catch your attention. You may also call, with your heart, for an animal to be with you. Don't worry if you don't see one at first, just stay with the experience. Be gentle with yourself as you explore. These tentative reaches into the Lowerworld may feel like your first baby steps as a child. Have compassion for yourself and allow these precious sensations to exist without judgment.

When you meet an animal, get acquainted. Spend time learning its ways, following it, speaking with it. You may discover, over the course of a few journeys, that you are met by the same animal or bird each time you enter the Lowerworld. You may feel a powerful connection to that spirit. It may impart knowledge to you or give you a healing. These are reliable signs that you have a new ally. This spirit being may be a power animal for you. If you feel this is the case, you may, of course, ask the animal in order to be certain.

When the call-back signal calls you to return, thank those beings you met on your journey and quickly retrace your path back to this reality.

Once you have returned to ordinary reality, breathe and give yourself time to reflect on your experience. It is important to record the journey in your journal. This helps to fix the information and experiences in your mind. Pay particular attention to the interactions you had with your new animal friend. In subsequent journeys, you may have further interactions with this animal. Once a spirit animal becomes a consistent companion and advisor, it is referred to as a "power animal."

The relationship with your power animal will provide you with many irreplaceable moments and gifts. Once you feel comfortable with a power animal, it's easier to venture safely and more deeply into other realms. Having a reliable and steady companion allows you more freedom to stretch your perceived limits, while retaining your feelings of safety. Human beings take new steps far more readily when they have a hand (or paw or wing) to hold.

Power animals may also be called upon here in the Middleworld for protection, strength, and assistance. My power animal has kept me company in several very fearful and stressful situations. I have consistently felt supported through many of life's ordeals by simply asking for its help. For me, power animals have become my most reliable source of personal, spiritual "octane boosting," giving me the extra courage and stamina to make it through anything that comes my way.

Remember, too, that it is in the Lowerworld, that you will begin the renewal of your hunter/gatherer sensibilities. In relating to the spirits of the animals, plants, birds, and other spirits of the natural world, we awaken our more ancient selves who understand that everything around us is alive. We are able to see again the interconnectedness of all of creation.

As we enter the Lowerworld, we also enter into a re-evolution toward the process paradigm. The journey process itself is an excellent reminder. Experienced journeyers often say that, the more they learn, the more journeys they are led to undertake, and the more questions they think to ask! In other words, the process of interacting with the spirits is a process of endless, unfolding possibilities.

1. *Spend some time thinking about the experiences you had with your power animal. You may want to write about this. Many people find that moving like, or dancing with the energy of, the animal is an extraordinarily powerful way to concretize the experience. It is also an excellent way to honor your animal's spirit.*

2. *How do you feel about meeting this animal?*

3. *Describe its perceived attributes or "powers."*

4. *What other creatures or plants did you see on your journey? Make some notes.*

Working with your Power Animal

When you have developed a firm relationship with your power animal, you will want to ask its advice about many things. In order to receive clear information, it is useful to enter into this dialog with a clear inquiry.

First of all, it is important to take the time to ask yourself what it is you truly wish to know. Often, when we think about a line of questioning, we shift our original ideas about what we want to know. Let me give an example.

You may want to find out about a job. Do you want to ask about the type of position, the sort of company, the physical place of employment, the "rightness" of the work? Always consider first what specific information is most important to you.

Once you narrow the category, word your question so that the answer will be clear. There are certain types of questions that seem to get the best results. These are usually questions that begin with

How . . . Where . . . What . . . Why . . . or *Who . . . .* So, if you have narrowed your work-issue question to one about the working environment, you might ask: "What company will provide the best workplace for me?" Or: "Where is the best place for me to work?" But be careful. That question could raise the issue of changing locations as well as jobs. You can see how important it is to figure out what kind of information would be most useful.

It is also important to keep your questions simple and to ask only one question per journey! You can always do another journey to get further details. Remember: this is a process. As you ask questions and receive answers about an issue, your focus may shift. You may find yourself going off in an entirely new direction based on the information you receive. That, for me, is part of the magic of journeying.

It is always important to remember that the information you receive on a journey is yours to act on or *not* to act on. Under no circumstance is it necessary or required to give up your power of choice—your precious free will—to any other being and that includes the spirits. You are a precious part of creation, no more or less important than any other!

My teacher spirits have shared a wonderful image with me to remind me of this truth. They used the metaphor of a ball game. We humans are sitting down very close to the field, where we can see hand signals and the subtle expressions on the player's faces. The spirits sit farther up in the stadium, where the intricate patterns of the plays are more obvious. We simply have different perspectives on the same game. When we seek the advice of spirits, we are asking for their perspective—the blimp's-eye view of our life process. Even when we ask for very concrete information about a situation here on the field, they are able to help us perceive the larger picture. We, in turn, offer the spirits a chance to interact with us and the physical plane. Our relationship to the spirits evolves, in this process, to one of profound respect, without hierarchy.

This is consistent with our shift to the hunter mind. We, through this adventure, perceive other humans, animals, plants, and the planet itself as equally important. *All* are necessary elements in life's formula. The following questions will get you started.

1. *How do you wish me to honor our connection? Remember, this is a relationship. Your power animal deserves respect and honor for its assistance. It may wish you to honor it with a photo in your room or ask it to be part of your thoughts when you pray. Be open.*

2. *What are the powers of the seasons? You may ask about each season individually.*

3. *In what ways, of which I am unaware, do I change when the seasons change?*

4. *How is my [life, work, relationship, health] process affected by where I live? (Choose one.)*

5. *What spirits in the natural world are important allies in helping me better understand the process paradigm?*

6. *What phase of the Moon helps support me to make the changes I'm ready for? (You may have a specific process topic.)*

7

Journeying to the Upperworld

|t is most common to find human-shaped spirits in the Upperworld. These spirit teachers are available to answer our questions, guide our steps, and encourage our own inherent inner wisdom. These spirit beings may range from the spirits of wise people who once lived, to those we think of as mythical. In each case, it is the highest spiritual energy of that being that we encounter in the Upperworld. These are the spirits who have made the transition into the highest planes of existence and who are, therefore, the safest sources of knowledge in a recognizably human form. It is just as possible to meet a teacher who was once a living person, such as Gandhi, Moses, or your great grandmother, as it is to meet a form such as Kwan Yin, Neptune, Tinkerbell, or a star being.

It is my belief that the spirits take a form that is most useful for our interactions. For instance, when we teach people how to journey, they are often surprised by who appears in the Upperworld to meet them. People with Jewish backgrounds have been met by Buddha, atheists have been met by Jesus, and others by W. C. Fields! And each of these spirits in the

Upperworld gives extraordinary guidance. There appears to be no spiritual hierarchy in the Upperworld. Spirits in this place are representatives, capable of providing universal knowledge and wisdom.

For your first Upperworld experience, set aside a quiet time and space, as you did for your other journeys. Take some time to formulate a journey question, using the question formats found in the previous chapter. Keeping the inquiry clear and simple is best for journey work. Also, don't forget to write down your question. This will help you to remember your journey purpose.

Once you are settled and have a question, start the drumming tape. Begin your Upperworld journey in your power-filled place. Look around for a way to ascend. This way may be a tree, a mountain, a golden ladder, a hot-air balloon, even a kite string. You may find it possible simply to rise into the sky from your power spot. Continue to give yourself permission to have this new experience. When you have found your own personal pathway to the Upperworld, begin to travel upward.

At some point, as you climb, you will reach a barrier or membrane. Just as you had to pass through the boundary of the Earth itself to enter the Lowerworld, so, too, you must pass through this barrier that separates the Middleworld from the realm of the Upperworld. This barrier may present itself as a rubbery membrane, a distinct ceiling of mist, or a parchmentlike surface. Move yourself through this barrier and into the Upperworld.

When you arrive in this place, take time to observe your surroundings. What do you perceive? Is there a landscape? Are there buildings or structures of some kind? Just as you did in your Lowerworld journeys, use all of your senses to explore this realm. If you wish, call to the power animal that you met in the Lowerworld to help you explore this wonder-filled place. Move around and keep looking for a teacher in human form. Remember, this is an active practice.

Immediately upon meeting any being, ask: Are you my teacher? If this spirit being doesn't answer clearly in the affirmative, continue on your journey until you find the right teacher for your question. Always clarify if a spirit is the teacher for your journey question. This way you can more fully trust his or her responses. After you receive an affirmative response, you may ask your journey question. Be patient. You are worthy of receiving clear information!

After you have asked your question, allow the teacher to reveal the answer to you. Your question may be answered by the whole rest of the journey, particularly if your teacher answers in metaphors. Your teacher may speak directly to you. You may experience a journey within a journey. Whatever it is, just allow the process to unfold before you. Remember, you will always have the choice to follow this advice or not, as your own personal guidance suggests. You never need to relinquish your free will.

When the call-back sounds, thank your teacher for his or her assistance and return to ordinary reality.

Spend as much time as you require reentering this reality. Remember the question and the answer you received. Write down as much of your journey as you can recall.

The information you receive in the Upperworld can be quite concrete! Here is a personal example of this that I would like to share.

When I was learning how to use the journey process as a way to help others, I wanted assurance that it really was a reliable way to gain insight about issues that were difficult or even impossible to solve using ordinary reality methods. (I attribute this to my concrete Taurean personality!)

For most of my adult life, I had tried to find out how to recreate my great, great grandmother Henderer's drawing salve. She had been an herbal doctor in the early part of the 20th century, and was taught the "old ways" of healing by her German mother. During the course of her lifetime, many changes took place in New York, especially in the arenas of sanitation and health. The hospitals became cleaner and new services, such as visiting nursing care, became available. As a result, the herbal knowledge that had been passed down for generations was no longer perceived as useful. Science was becoming the way of medicine.

Because of the pro-scientific prejudice, she found herself unable to pass on the old healing ways. Even her seven children, all possible apprentices, thought those ways were too old-fashioned. Perhaps she herself had lost faith in their ability to hold their own against the tide of new medicines. For whatever reasons, her remedies were not shared, nor were they written down. The recipes were lost to time once she died.

One of the many medicines that Grandma had made was still being used when I was a child. In our linen closet was a rusty-topped old canning jar that was taken out when any of the family had a bad cut. It contained the last of Grandma's drawing salve. It was especially relied upon when a wound became infected. No over-the-counter salve worked as fast or as completely! It drew out infections overnight. And it's unusual, but very pleasant, smell was unlike anything else in the world.

During the Great Depression, when my father was a child, he stepped on a rusty nail. Having little money, his family used the salve on his foot, hoping to avoid a trip to the hospital. The salve not only cleared out the infection, it was discovered the next morning that the salve had actually drawn out the rust itself from the wound!

In the early 1960s my family tried to find out the ingredients of the salve by taking small amounts of the precious stuff to a chemist. While the chemist was able to identify the compounds that were present, the technology of that time was unable to recreate the recipe, since the salve's compounds were created by altering the original ingredients through cooking. Ironically, the science that had replaced Grandma's ways was unable to help reconstruct her salve. During the course of my childhood, the last of it was used up.

I had, over many years, done extensive research on herbal salves, hoping to find a recipe that could recreate this family treasure. I made lots of salve, but none like Grandma's. That recipe remained elusive. So, to really put the journey process to the test, I decided to try to discover the lost secrets of Grandma Henderer.

Over the course of a week's journeying, I was able to actually meet the spirit of Grandma in the Upperworld and have her teach me how to make her salve.

Once back at home, I set about gathering the ingredients she had shared with me in my journeys.

This took awhile, as many of the necessary components, though quite common and easily accessible in Grandma's time, were a little tricky to get today. (For instance, rosin that she could buy in a corner drugstore was only available to me in the form of violin-bow dressing!)

After a bit of struggle, I finally took a Saturday out of my life and got to work. I hadn't realized how important this experience was to me until I started the process of preparing the salve. I was perspiring, even though the kitchen was still quite cool!

Cooking the ingredients took all day. After watching them simmer for almost seven hours, I strained the resulting dark, greasy, and hot liquid through cheesecloth into a canning jar. Then I waited until morning.

When I awoke the next morning, I could smell the aromas left from the previous day's labor. They pulled me into the kitchen. There on the stove top was a jar of golden-colored salve. I raised it to my nose and was greeted by an aroma that was unmistakable. Grandma's salve!

Of course, I had to wait until I had an infected cut to make sure that it worked like her salve. After many months of gathering, cooking, and waiting, I finally knew it was right. It worked just like the salve that my family and I remembered. And I, joyfully, had confirmed the journey process.

As you practice journeying, each of you will receive a similarly irrefutable confirmation that helps you to trust more fully in the invisible world. Be persistent, be patient. Hold to the process, and trust that those moments will arrive.

You may have journey questions for either a teacher or your power animal. The following suggestions may help you work with your journal.

1. *What parts of my life processes are invisible to me?*

2. *What are the things in my life that can aid me most in my personal growth?*

3. *How am I affected by my own fears?*

4. *What are the steps to becoming less attached to goals?*

5. *What are the steps to understanding my life as a process paradigm?*

6. *What are the interferences that I create in my own process paradigm?*

7. *Are there other people around who are interfering with my life process?*

8. *How do my desires affect the nature of my life?*

Journeying to Meet the Inner Hunter

Our familiarity with the Otherworlds gives us a place to begin the work of actually meeting with our inner hunter. Spirit beings may be anywhere and everywhere, since they are not restrained by the limits of physical form. These unlimited, fluid essences may also be in more than one place simultaneously. According to the shamanic perspective, we are *filled with spirit.* Moreover, our own spirits have the capacity to be in more than one place at a time. Our culture refers to this as multidimensionality. This makes it possible for us to meet a being in the Otherworld who is still living.

This multidimensional, human ability allows us to engage with a part of ourselves as though it were a separate being. In the Otherworld, we can actually meet this inner hunter and take tentative steps toward a partnership that gives us conscious access to his or her gifts.

Once you are centered and ready to begin this journey, call your power animal to you in the Middleworld by calling out with your heart as well as your mind. Once you feel connected, start your journey process in your power spot, but allow your power animal to guide you to the appropriate realm—to either Upperworld or Lowerworld. Your intention will be to meet with your inner hunter as a teacher. Having your power animal along from the very start of this journey will assist you in getting clear information. Most people find that having a trusted spirit along when embarking on new spiritual experience gives them more confidence.

Once you are clearly in the Lowerworld or Upperworld, call out in your mind to the hunter/gatherer that is inside you to reveal him- or herself. Let go of any preconceived notion of how this part may appear. If you wish, you may ask your animal's help in calling this being to you. Again, as with every other journey, be both patient and persistent. Keep calling out to and searching for this being, until you begin to perceive its presence.

You may suddenly be aware of another person nearby or have the experience of seeing the hunter manifest right in front of you. Let it happen however it needs to happen, without judging the process.

As you did in the Upperworld journeys, ask this being: "Are you my teacher?" Since your intention is to meet your inner hunter/gatherer, an affirmative answer to this question will clarify who this is.

Once you have received an affirmative response, you may wish to begin with a question like, "What is important for you to share with me, at this time?" This question offers the spirit an opportunity to teach you what is most appropriate in your process. Another line of inquiry might be, "How can I become more conscious of you in my daily life?" This question can provide an excellent entry opportunity into what will hopefully become a powerful relationship.

Relationship is a key word. In view of our shifting paradigm, the idea of relationship implies a multifaceted process that is dynamic and always evolving. In other words, you will not be best served by meeting only once or twice with this part of yourself. Instead, this inner being must become an active part of your support network. This is made possible by this powerful shamanic journey method. Accessing this inner hunter offers you the possibility for real transformation of yourself and, therefore, of the culture and the planet.

Change does not have to be traumatic. With the aid of this inner character, we can relish all the changes we move through in our lives without fear or judgment. Change is the hunter's constant companion. Yet, even in the face of constant change, this being holds firm, avoids fear, and keeps moving ahead. We have so much we can learn from the hunter/gatherer. We need only be willing to keep asking the questions and following through with our growing wisdom.

You may have journey questions for your inner hunter after you have read this section. The following list of questions may help you work through the process.

1. *How can I become more conscious of you in my daily life?*

2. *Where in my life are you already active?*

3. *What do you need from me?*

4. *Who are my most supportive allies?*

5. *What would assist me in getting to know you better?*

6. *How often would it be most useful for me to meet with you? Ask this question seasonally.*

7. *How do I become less fearful of change?*

8. *How can you help me be more in tune with the Earth?*

9. *How can I perceive the "big picture?"*

10. *How can you help me be more aware of shifting energies?*

11. *How do I become more fluid? (Or more able to flow with the process.)*

12. *What is your understanding of the universe?*

The Body as a Partner

As a culture, we are awakening to a new conceptual understanding of the body, its systems, and our health. Through exposure to science programs on television and through health-related articles, we are beginning to recognize the truths of our physical form. Each of us, as individual organisms, is as delicately balanced as the Earth itself. We have, inside our bodies, complex systems that are as prone to disturbance as any outside ecosystem.

Through our wish to control the surface of our world, we have made our human needs preeminent. In our dominion over the Earth, we have made all other creatures' needs and the long-term health of the land itself subordinate to our own. The results of this folly can be seen everywhere. For instance, whole regions of Africa, inhabited just a few decades ago, have become hostile places with spreading deserts. In our great collective impertinence, we have implemented countless changes. In this same manner of thinking that "we know best," we have used our minds to subjugate the needs and will of our physical bodies.

Through the tragedy of the global AIDS crisis and the horrific, widespread occurrences of cancer in our culture, we have learned that the health and function of the human immune system reflects the overall health of our inner ecology. In addition, we are seeing that it is no longer possible for many of us to force our bodies to *do* what we want them to do. We see even young bodies pulled down by chronic, fatiguing illnesses. This appears to be part of our species' lesson about hierarchical thinking and behavior. We no longer have the option to dominate our bodies with our minds. The idea of pushing through our limitations—"no pain, no gain"—is no longer generally operational. Sure, we can get away with that behavior for a time, but, if we are honest, if we listen to our bodies, they are asking us to perceive them in a different way.

We are guilty of this hierarchical behavior in our spiritual life as well. We have used the will of the spirit to hold sway over our minds and bodies. In the past, it was universally understood that the pursuit of true spiritual growth meant the denial of the flesh. Entire religious systems support this belief. In the illusions of our old paradigm, we thought we could simply rise above the supposedly base needs of the organism. For centuries, we have given our bodies the message that they are somehow an impediment to the spirit! And yet, don't our religious texts tell us these remarkable containers were made in the image of God? Doesn't that infer that our human bodies are therefore also a part of the divine?

We are beginning to see that, what we have done to subjugate the Earth, we have also done to ourselves. And it is clear, for meaningful, sustained, and healthy change to occur, that we must enter into a collaboration with *all* the components of ourselves and the world around us.

What makes this new behavior such a struggle, at least at first, is that we do not understand how the body communicates. The body does not communicate with words or thoughts. Language is a late evolutionary step. The body "speaks" in an older, more universal communication style—the symbolic "language" of imagery and sensation. It speaks to us in this manner almost constantly, but we aren't usually listening. This forces the body to communicate in a more forceful way in order to have it's needs met.[1]

How many of us have needed rest and refused to honor our fatigue? Perhaps we felt that we couldn't take time off, yet, when we fell ill, we took an entire week of sick time! We left the body no other choice but to shout at us through the development of an illness. This is not meant to lay the blame for our diseases soley on us. But we must begin to recognize that our immune systems are under a constant onslaught. Our environment has become, to a great degree, toxic to our bodies. We have altered our air, water, and soil—and, therefore, our inner environments—to a frightening extent. At this juncture, we are like the painter who has painted himself into a corner. We need help to get out of our dilemma. By entering into a deep collaboration with all of creation, we can have the assistance we need.

Speaking with the body can be an extraordinarily humbling experience. Let me share a powerful example

---

[1] Arnold Mindell, *The Shaman's Body* (New York: HarperCollins, 1993), pp. 103–107.

of this process from my own life. My first genuine dialogue with my body began when I strove to understand a disease. I had developed severe pelvic pain and bleeding. I was diagnosed with a condition called DUB, or dysfunctional uterine bleeding. After ultrasound and other tests, it became clear there were several things amiss in my pelvic region, the most dramatic of these being huge ovarian cysts. Somehow, my body decided to grow foreign objects on my ovaries. What did this mean?

As part of the discussions with my physicians about cause and treatments, it became very clear to me that it was necessary to ask my body and my ovaries what was going on. Even though I had received the advice of medical professionals about my condition, I still needed to hear what my own body had to tell me.

A journey into the body, either for diagnosis or dialog, may be undertaken in several ways. The way I usually prefer to begin is by going to my primary teacher in the Upperworld. This is the spirit who has consistently given me the clearest information. After asking my teacher for help, we then descend together to the Middleworld and enter my body. Sometimes, we shrink down and enter the top of my head. Sometimes we simply sink down into the inner body's realm.

Once inside, we ask the sentient being of the body if there is a particular spokesperson for the question. Often, a single organ speaks for the body. At other times, the collective voice of the physical form speaks. You may have a different process, so be patient if it takes a little time to clarify your own personal situation. The information gained in this journey will be invaluable and well worth the effort.

Once a spokesperson has been revealed, you may ask your question. Choose your question based on what you most want to know. A great "icebreaker question" in these situations is, "What do you wish to communicate to me about this condition?" This is sufficiently open-ended to allow the body to communicate whatever it wishes and to give you insight into the illness.

The spokesperson for my journey into the body was my right ovary. The ovary showed me that my body had become overwhelmed with a task I myself had given it! A few years prior, I had asked my body to release any unbeneficial fear and any generators of fear that existed in my body. During the course of my transition into a more conscious lifestyle, I had done a great deal of work on transcending those limiting, fear-driven messages from family and culture, but I still felt fear's power to interfere with my existence.

Since, unknown to my conscious mind, I was still operating under a goal-centered model, I believed it was possible to remove the generators of fear and, voila!, I'd be clearer and healthier. I had, in my human impatience, forgotten about the idea of process.

Now my ovary, a generator organ, swelled with these cysts as it tried to rid my body of my fear generators. The cysts were, in part, due to my own seemingly healthy request. Yet, even in this overwhelmed state, my ovary did not judge me! Quite the contrary, it told me it was grateful for the chance to speak with me. It went on to communicate how it wished to proceed with the recommended surgery, as the strain of the cysts was causing other systems to suffer. So much of my body's energy was engaged in stabilizing the area, that the body could not correct an underlying hormonal imbalance that was beginning to cascade symptoms all over my body.

At the end of the journey, I thanked the ovary for its hard work and asked how else I could support it and the rest of my body. It gave me a few suggestions and then said something quite unexpected. It told me, "I will communicate your willingness to speak with the body to the universal body matrix."

Just as Carl Jung suggested that there was a collective unconscious, my ovary was referring to a bodily equivalent! At that moment, I realized that I was part of an even bigger process than I had originally thought. I knew that my body and its symptoms could become my allies. I was no longer fighting against a disease. I was working inside a huge process in which I only had to do my part—keeping the lines of communication, and, therefore, healing, open.

With this new understanding that health was not a static goal, but a process, I no longer had to wait until I was more healthy to follow my soul's purpose. Instead, I realized this symptom was part of my soul's journey. While I certainly had to give my body more of my time, it didn't mean losing anything. As long as health was part of the journey, the time given over to the body was not any sort of sacrifice. I was still free to create artwork, teach, go to the beach, journey—all the things I loved to do—as long as I listened to what my body wished as well. This was the beginning of my conscious understanding of the process paradigm.

Subsequent journeys revealed more about how the human body matrix is assaulted by our old ways of thinking. My body told me it was suffering from a hormonal imbalance that was aggravated by external sources of hormones. In these journeys, I was shown that my body's endocrine system was affected by various chemicals in my food, air, and water. These chemicals acted as endocrine disrupters. Pesticides, herbicides, cleaners, chemicals used to accelerate growth in cattle, and many other industrial compounds were being interpreted by my body as simulants of natural estrogen! It became clear, through these journeys, that, in order to further assist my body, I needed to find out more about these external hormone sources. More information would assist me in changing my way of thinking, my way of living, and my way of eating.

This journey information was confirmed for me when I read *Women's Bodies, Women's Wisdom*. In it, Dr. Christiane Northrup, holistic physician and women's health pioneer, suggests this externally sourced, dietary estrogen as a contributing factor in conditions ranging from uterine fibroids, ovarian cancer, breast cancer, and several other hormone-sensitive diseases.[2]

Then, through the marvel of the World Wide Web, I accessed all I could find on endocrine disrupters. From web sites as diverse as the World Wildlife Fund, Canada[3] and the U.S. Environmental Protection Agency,[4] I discovered that the list of these toxic compounds is very extensive and that they pervade much of our lives!

---

[2] Christiane Northrup, *Women's Bodies, Women's Wisdom* (New York: Bantam Books, 1994), p. 592.
[3] www.wwfcanada.org (World Wildlife Fund, Canada's web site). The WWF, Canada, offers several well-researched, easy-to-understand pamphlets and a video to assist in identifying and reducing exposure to these many pollutants. Their phone number is 1-800-26-PANDA.
[4] www.epa.gov

These substances affect the body by mimicking, blocking, stimulating, flushing out, or simply destroying the body's natural hormones. Our hormones are produced in the collection of glands known as the endocrine system. These hormones are released into our bloodstream, where they work in extraordinarily complex ways to regulate our many body systems. Hormones get their name from the Greek word meaning "to urge on." They "urge," or regulate, everything from our ability to digest foods, to providing our "fight or flight response," to regulating our immune response, or determining our gender.

The healthy body produces our natural hormones in quite tiny amounts. For instance, natural estrogen operates at a concentration that is measured in parts per trillion. Our bodies are often contaminated with levels of estrogen-mimicking compounds in levels measured in parts per billion or parts per million. These levels are a thousand to a million times greater than our naturally occurring hormone levels![5] Imagine the possible havoc these levels can wreak on our body's ability to maintain a healthy system.

Some of these endocrine-disrupting agents are:

Nonylphenol ethoxylates (NPE), found in detergents, as additives in latex paint, and in cosmetics and even spermacides.

Persistent organic pollutants (POPs), such as dioxin (a by-product of many chemical processes involving chlorine, such as bleaching paper, and a common contaminant in vinyl plastics, such as PVC), PCBs,

---

[5] Theo Colburn, Diane Dumanoski, and John Peterson Myers, *Our Stolen Future* (New York: Penguin Books, 1997), p. 74.

DDT (DDT breaks down to DDE in our systems, producing birth defects similar to those found among people whose mothers were given DES), and pentachlorophenol, a wood preservative.

Heavy Metals, such as lead, mercury, and cadmium. These are found in diverse sources such as batteries, old lead paint, tooth fillings, and cigarettes.[6]

My research suggested changing many parts of my life to eliminate or reduce exposure to these harmful agents, including: eating only organic produce; eating lower on the food chain to reduce exposure to the levels of pollutants found in fatty animal products like meat, dairy products, and eggs; eliminating NPE-contaminated cleaners, shampoos, and bleached paper products; avoiding plastics as much as possible (especially eliminating the practice of microwaving food in plastic containers), and eliminating pesticide, herbicide, and fungicide use in the home and yard.[7]

The information I was learning through dialoguing with my body and through my research felt so important to me that I found I was sharing it with others. I realized that, instead of remaining at the mercy of a disease—instead of being a victim—I was learning incredible things and moving my energy into action on behalf of myself. And, as is generally the case, I found that what I experienced and knew best,

---

[6] www.wwfcanada.org (World Wildlife Fund, Canada's website). The WWF, Canada, offers several well-researched, easy-to-understand pamphlets and a video to assist in identifying and reducing exposure to these many pollutants. Their phone number is 1-800-26-PANDA.

[7] *Reducing Your Risk: A Guide to Avoiding Hormone-Disrupting Chemicals*, pp. 7–12. Informational pamphlet produced by the World Wildlife Fund in Canada, 1997.

was what I could best teach! Talk about a shift in perspective!

These journeys gave me an especially positive understanding of how my particular body processes were reacting to all these substances. That understanding, along with the concrete suggestions from my body, as well as the advice offered by my doctors, gave me a perspective that I equate with the hunter's "big picture" viewpoint. In addition, I knew I had to stay in contact with my body to monitor my progress, since this situation, like all others, was, of course, a process!

Whatever your particular health situation, I believe that journeying into the body can provide you with very useful knowledge. If you are ill, your body can show you how you may be vibrantly alive while in the middle of a profound healing process. Shifting our perceptions and our worldview to the hunter's process-centered model allows joy to unfold in *any* circumstance. When we are able to see all of our experiences as processes that are intertwined, we are freed from the emotional pains that usually accompany illness. Instead of waiting patiently (or, as with my case, impatiently) to get well, we are assured by our own bodies that we are in a flow that is always dynamic and changing. And, as my partner often says, "It beats suffering!"

Even apparently healthy people can benefit from journeying into the body. Consider the idea of being able to dialogue with one of your cells. Imagine the information you could access about topics such as the possible effects of foods or medications. Imagine actually asking your body what supplements it requires to remain fit, or how it wishes to exercise. You could determine how much sleep your body requires, where it would feel most at home, what aspects of your life actually help it to function at an optimum level, or discover what amazing stories it has to share with you.

I recommend that, whether you perceive yourself as in vigorous health, suffering a debilitating illness, or in simply average physical condition, it can be useful for you to enter into a dialogue with your body. There is a wealth of extraordinary, unimaginably rich knowledge—that can, in fact, be seen as *divine* wisdom—in every one of your miraculous cells.

These are a number of questions you can ask of your inner hunter in this stage of working with yourself. Hopefully, the questions mentioned below will get you started.

1. *Ask your inner hunter how your body is connected to the Earth.*

2. *Also ask if your body changes inside, as the seasons change in the outside world.*

3. *What foods (or supplements) would be most beneficial during this season?*

4. *If you have a teacher, ask how you can begin the process of perceiving your body as an ally.*

5. *Can your teacher help you learn the ways in which you are affected by the people around you?*

6. *What does your teacher want you to change in your diet? Ask about such topics as shifting to organic produce, eating dairy products, how your body is affected by ingesting meat, or other things*

about which you are curious. Remember, you don't have to rely only on what you read or see on TV—ask your own body!

7. *Ask your teacher about how a specific situation affects your body, i.e., your particular job, your place of work, living arrangement, etc.*[8]

8. *What are my symptoms trying to communicate?*

9. *How can I assist you in your healing process?*

The Mesa Ceremony (A Shamanic Journey Dream Story)

A late October chill is creeping over the the land and a mist, nearly as heavy as rain, is dripping from the bowing trees. Clouds obscure the heavens. Time and place blend seductively in this atmosphere without Moon or stars. The mind worries, as we fall between the cracks of understanding.

Inside the barn, the darkness is folding its way around a circle of people. Huddling together, cradling their fears and pains, they have gathered in this netherworld. Shivering with more than the cold demands, they await midnight, when the healing ceremony begins.

The air is filled with the exotic scents of rum, herbs, incense, and perfume. The incense curls up in

---

[8] This was a real eye-opening journey for me. I was reminded about my body's daily need for sunlight and the illusions we still hold about our skin's imperviousness. The body showed me the stop-smoking patch that is a transdermal delivery system for nicotine. Then the body showed me all the man-made chemicals with which we routinely come in contact every day: detergent, makeup, hand cream, gasoline (when I fill my car), paint, pesticides (on fruit), even nail polish. The inference was that I should consciously consider what I allowed on my skin, since some of those chemicals were entering my body.

gray ribbons in front of the curandero and his assistants. These three, seated behind the altar, are here to work magic. They are the Center. It is their responsibility to hold the forces of light and shadow as spirits fill the mesa.

Arranged around the low surface of the altar are many objects. Hardly perceptible in the gloom, the weapons of slaughter nestle beside the bones of saints. Bottles, filled with things barely seen, tempt a closer inspection—an incentive quickly dispelled by the anxiety of knowing their contents. Beautiful, terrible relics with fresh flowers—all holy—in balance. And these many things begin their awakening under the curandero's song. His spell snakes through the smoke, coaxing spirits into form, playing the mysteries in their eternal variations.

Forming gestures and chanting prayers, the three bless the containers of sacred remedy, squatting, thick and green, in the earthen jugs on the floor. Weaving their words into each other's, they raise strangely shaped shells containing a much darker liquid. Following the curandero's signal, the assistants bring the shells to their faces while he sings. Tipping their heads up in unison, they pour the potion into their nostrils. Strong with perfume, tobacco, and other unspoken scents, this fluid careens through their heads and down their throats. Instantly, their minds are snapped into clarity by its powerful charm. All is ready for the long night of visions that will assault their eyes. Solemnly picking up the jugs of potent cactus, they pour the liquid into cups that they drain quickly. The sacrament is then shared with those who have nervously waited in the circle.

Quietly at first, the song that will usher in the magic begins.

When eyes begin to open beyond the blackness of the barn, the curandero raises his voice above the rest. The time has arrived for those who wish the assistance of the spirits to step forward.

The people stand, each in turn, quivering to the front of the altar to make their requests. The healers, surrounded by the chattering of their invisible spirit companions, look first into the hearts of those who stand before them. Staring at silhouettes in the vibrating darkness, they search for light and shadow. Spirits fill the air around the supplicants with dancing shades they must interpret.

And so, they see.

This young man is dying. Once muscular, he stands before the three as a man now thin and vulnerable. Clearly, the illness has wrecked havoc with his body, yet it has not ravaged his spirit in the same way. His voice is strong as he prays for healing.

Slowly, objects on the mesa begin their murmuring in response to his earnest request. A single tool must show itself apart from the rest. Locked in concentration, the three behind the altar become one. Holding hands, linking their own spirits for the purpose before them, they are flooded with power.

Finally, a minute and forever later, they see the one object that lies glowing in front of them. Picking up the sword of St. Michael, the curandero walks out from his place behind the mesa. An assistant quickly fills his chair so that the fulcrum may be balanced.

Upon reaching the center of the room, the patient and the healer become shadows swaying in the circle. Slicing the air around the man, the curandero frees him first from the fear that surrounds him. This smothering shroud drops away, slithering back into the huge pool of fear that centuries of humans have created. He prays continuously as he works, and all three of the visionaries follow the elaborate choreography laid out for them by Spirit. They see tiny, jibbering monstrosities and hear a terrible shrieking and mumbling unheard by the rest. And they feel compassion, even for this illness itself. They know all spirits have a place in creation. It is balance that must be regained. Intentions and actions waltz around as part of the dance. None are separate. No one less important.

Past and future ages are parading through the now-transparent body of the man. In shifts almost too rapid to see, he is a marching centurion and nursing mother. He is, at once, a child, an old woman, and a prince—now, in this present moment. And this vision, too, is part of the healing. With cactus-cleared eyes, everyone in the circle sees themselves as endless, precious elements in a complex formula.

Three healers, still as one, grasp the center, as the edges fall away. They can taste every image as it blurs past. People of the circle begin to change. Their bodies first stretch up, then rush toward the myriad stars that now surround the mesa. The fabric of their bodies strains and sounds wrap every cell, as reality drowns in new possibilities.

And, just as suddenly, floors and walls regain their place as the barn shimmers back. The young man is crawling to his feet, wiping tears from his smiling face. Those closest help him to his seat, as the curandero returns to his work.

The three take hands again. There are more who are ready to come forward, until the dawn sends spirits scattering back to their invisible realms. Yet, even unseen, it will continue. This game of eternal balancing and flowing is the essence of the universe. Endless and joyful.

And when the people set about eating and laughing with the rising Sun, they will know they have witnessed miracles that do not depend on anyone being cured. The path of miracles rolls out before us with every step we make in harmony with the rest of creation.

9

Traveling the Path Together

Dr. Andrew Weil suggests that full health cannot be experienced when we perceive ourselves as isolated, separate beings. He argues that health itself refers to a wholeness that includes connectedness. This connection must extend beyond our immediate family and friends to the community, the Earth, and, indeed, even to Spirit.[1] I would add further that it is not possible for the Earth to return to health unless we recognize the need for these connections.

The word "connection" implies relationship. We cannot hope to flow with the rest of creation unless we enter into deep connections with other human beings. These relationships, beginning first within our own species, give us the tools to manifest a shift toward a balanced, harmonious existence with all living creatures.

This entrance into a new understanding of relationship requires us first to recognize that the needs of others are equal to our own. This sounds simple, yet, in practice, the hierarchical struggles for power

---

[1] Andrew Weil, *Natural Health, Natural Medicine* (Boston: Houghton Mifflin Co., 1990), p. 149.

within a relationship are precisely what keeps them mired in dysfunction. It is important to note that my definition of relationship includes those between friends, siblings, colleagues, parents with their children, and other close associations, in addition to what we recognize as intimate partnerships. The way we behave in these relationships has a direct bearing on how our world works. Remember, humans create the culture in which they live. If we structure our interpersonal existences in hierarchical and compartmentalized ways, we structure the world around us in this same image. It therefore becomes necessary to start the process of changing our outer world by altering our societal structure at home.

Before you are overwhelmed at the immensity of the task, look at the elements of exactly how a relationship can be shifted toward the hunter's more fluid model. Remember that relationship itself—as with all other things we've looked at thus far—is a *process*. We have already looked at how we are constantly in process, as individuals. Relationships, too, are dynamic organisms meant to grow, change, and evolve as the situations that create their contexts shift. When we create a fixed model—a compartment—for what we believe any relationship should be, we begin to manifest its ultimate demise. Like a species that is unable to evolve and adapt to climactic changes, anything static is doomed to fail. Nature is never still.

The idea of process seems to fly in the face of our current cultural definitions of relationship. Yet, if the available divorce statistics are any indicator, the current model seems to be a failure. Some suggest that, to remedy this failure, we need even stricter and more rigid benchmarks for relationship. But this seems ill conceived.

What would perhaps be more useful is for us to be *consciously in the process* of relationship. In the hunter's new world, nothing is taken for granted. For instance, the fact that a hunter may have been successful in finding game in the past did not ensure future success. As a result, the present moment was what was most relevant to a hunter. Each situation or interaction was therefore seen for itself—that is, it was largely removed from many of our limiting contexts.

If we assume this perspective, the roles we assume in our daily lives may become more flexible and compassionate and, as a result, our relationships may also become less limited. It is important to recognize that, in many cases, the preconceptions we have about relationship may be unconscious. Therefore, for this shift in perspective to result in more spontaneous and rewarding interactions, we must also make conscious adjustments in our behaviors. Many of these behaviors stem from our unconscious notions and preconceptions. (I recognize my own unconsciously driven actions as those I do as if I were "on automatic.")

In becoming more conscious, we realize that, in any moment, we have the ability to choose to act differently. This action, based on the parameters of a particular situation, must include the needs of the other in equal measure to our own needs. In order to determine what another's needs are in any situation—since they, too, are subject to evolution from one moment to the next—we must communicate with each other.

Communication is a skill that requires an equal measure of listening and speaking. In addition, when we speak and listen, we have to learn the art of nonjudgmental interaction. When we use judgmental words or tones with another, we create a power imbalance in our communication. Listening must also be undertaken without judgment. Recognize that, in order to assume a position of judgment, you must stand emotionally above another. This is a fundamentally hierarchical stance. This imbalance creates a reaction in our communication partner. In a reactive state, we can not be receptive to the communicated information. Therefore, the communication itself breaks down. In other words, in our attempt to control the situation by being emotionally above another, we have lost the vision of the *process* of communication.

Human communication also includes body language. This means that we must also be aware of *how* we are presenting ourselves during dialogue. Visual presentation is part of both listening and speaking. If our relationship partner wishes to speak with us, we need to make a conscious choice at that moment. If we wish real communication to occur, we must fully engage with that person. This includes physically looking at the person and assuming a receptive posture. If, on the other hand, we are unable to engage, it is our responsibility to articulate *that* information clearly to the other. It is not effective to relate only partially—listening, as it were, with only one ear. This telegraphs the impression that what the other person has to say is unimportant. Even if we are unable to engage at a particular moment due to fatigue or involvement in a task, we must respond clearly to the *request*. We must, at the very least, honor the equal worth of the other's thoughts.

When we choose not to engage, the communication partner also has a free choice. They may request us to refocus our attention on the task, or ask us when we will be able to be fully present. The entire interchange becomes a flow of conscious choices and responses. This dance of interactive respect can help to prevent the lingering resentments that can result due to an ineffective dialogue. These resentments contribute to the end of any possibility for an effective dialogue.

As you can see, in order to have a healthy relationship, we must see it as dynamic. In this dynamic model, every interaction becomes increasingly conscious. With some practice, this way of interacting also becomes less self-conscious!

In my own primary partnership, we have committed to undertake this paradigm shift with an air of experiment and adventure. We realize that, by looking at relationship in this way, we are, in effect, creating a model that has never existed before. As such, we are not limited by any of the precedents we have been given by our families of origin or our culture. We are free to evolve in a fully committed, joyful, and nonjudgmental environment. We realize that we create the relationship's parameters ourselves and, as such, we can, in any moment, do whatever works for both of us. We have learned that, as we continue to keep each other's needs equal to our own, we gain stronger trust in each other. In this atmosphere of trust, we can take emotional risks. This has created a bond between us more powerful than any preconceived, compartmentalized relationship structure could ever offer.

This same model is useful in all other relationships. Even if the other person is operating from the old paradigm, if we choose to communicate and act in the new way, we can break the old loop. When even one person in the relationship chooses to remain open in the face of a judgmental presentation or response, energy is not added to the dysfunction. We can shift the situation to a more balanced dialogue simply by not playing the game by the old rules!

In terms of the hunter's ability to hold the larger view in relationship, I believe that compassion is the most important part of the "big picture." This compassion must be present, not only for each other, but for ourselves. In our practice, we have seen that many people forget their own needs in the life equation. None of us can afford to be only caretakers. This is unbalanced. We must be cared for as well, and in equal measure. If our relationship partner is unable or unwilling to engage on equal footing, we must compassionately remove ourselves from the interaction. This is as simple as being able to say, in an argument, that you have to discuss this issue later, when both parties are able to listen. Remember, it takes two to escalate an argument and only one to diffuse a situation. If both parties want to retain a dynamic, growing relationship imbued with the larger vision of compassion, the relationship will flourish.

There are questions you'll need to ask to work all this information into your consciousness. A few questions follow to get you started.

1. *How do I keep from giving my personal responsibility in relationship, away to another?*

2. *In what ways, unseen to me, do I behave hierarchically?*

3. *What does a balanced relationship look like?*

4. *What did I learn about relationships from other people?*

5. *How do I contribute to my own happiness?*

6. *What are the steps to creating a new vision for my relationship with (insert a name)?*

7. *How am I taking over other people's relationship responsibilities?*

8. *How do my relationship interactions affect the Earth?*

10

Spiritual Ecology

THE RESULTS OF our disharmony with the environment are visible all around us. In 1989, the EPA reported that United States industries poured 4.57 billion pounds of chemicals into the nation's air, water, and soil.[1] This is just one country's record, for just one year. Moreover, this doesn't take into consideration that most of the pollutants that enter the environment come from households. Although the local superfund site may draw more attention, it is our own personal choices that affect the planet most profoundly.

Our nation's water supply is contaminated with pesticides in at least thirty-eight states. Thirty-five percent of the food consumed in the United States has detectable pesticide residues.[2] In many places, the nation's soils are too depleted for farming and air quality is still a major cause for concern. On certain days, it is considered unhealthy simply to breathe the air! Even in Maine, where much of the landscape is still undeveloped, we are subject to air pollution

---

[1] James A. Swan, *Nature as Teacher and Healer* (New York: Villard Books, 1992), p. xv.
[2] Theo Colburn, Diane Dumanoski, and John Peterson Myers, *Our Stolen Future* (New York: Penguin Books, 1997), p. 138.

alerts. Indeed, nowhere on Earth is free from our human actions and their resulting disharmony. No children born on this Earth, no matter in how remote a location, are born free from chemical contamination.[3]

These dire reports can give us a feeling of helplessness. In some cases, they cause a state of fear to overtake people. The emotion of fear itself is quite dangerous. It has been noted that fear is a toxic emotion. In fact, it is so toxic that intense fear can even kill. Both animals and humans are capable of being literally frightened to death.[4] So we cannot afford to simply be paralyzed and afraid. We must take action to find another path.

The Hopi use the word *akina* to refer to states of disharmony. In their view, this *akina* is only dispelled by intentional, harmonious action. While they are specifically referring to ritual, it is certainly true that *all* human actions must be undertaken in more harmonious and intentional ways.

We have already begun to act in a more intentional manner, as may be seen in the many, ongoing recycling and clean-up efforts across the country. Individuals, schools, and even some industries have begun to view the Earth and its systems in a more balanced way. We are beginning to be aware of the *genius loci*—the spirit of place.

The spirit of place is a collective expression that encompasses all the spirits that create the spiritual essence of an area. These essences include all the animals, plants, and natural features found in that

---

[3] Colburn, *Our Stolen Future*, p. 240.
[4] Carroll Izard, *Human Emotions* (New York: Plenum Press, 1977), p. 35.

place. As all are necessary components to the health, balance, and harmony of the place, we need to see them as parts of a whole.

When we refer to the spirit of place of the Rocky Mountains, for instance, we include all of the resident beings—the grizzly bear, the deer, the beaver, the hawk, the squirrel, the porcupine, the thrush, the eagle, the pine, and the rattlesnake—as well as the essence of the actual mountains themselves. If any of these parts of that ecosystem were missing, the *genius loci* would be altered.

As an even larger environment, our planet has a spirit of place as well. The Earth's spirit is the context in which all of the other spirits exist. Our ancestral, inner hunter/gatherer understands the world in this way. This spirit is held in our DNA. To affect the positive changes we desire, we must, therefore, *remember*. Remembering includes all that we have discovered thus far about the hunter. Remembering, as with all other things we've examined, is a process with many steps. Let's begin by going outside.

Most of us spend the majority of our lives in an indoor, synthetic environment. We go from house, to car, to work, and back again with no opportunity to really be *in* the world. In becoming detached from nature, we have fallen out of relationship with our larger home. It is, however, possible to remember our sacred connections. As with any relationship, we must learn how to communicate. To commune with the natural world, we have to begin by going into nature and introducing ourselves!

Go out into the space around your home. If it is possible, move away from the structure and any overhanging wires. Remember, even those of us who live in a dense urban setting can find a little bit of green—a tree, a patio container, or window box—that we can get to know better! *All* is important. No part of the Earth is spiritless.

In your outside space, take time to center yourself and breathe. Enter the grounded/expanded state. Notice what your senses perceive, both nearby and in the background. Give yourself as much time as you possibly can to do this exercise. Try to witness all that you perceive without judgment.

What do you see? What do you hear? What smells reach you? What color is the sky right now? Can you feel a breeze? From what direction is it blowing? In this moment, what creatures and plants are sharing the space with you? Give yourself permission to be acutely sensitive. Drink in all that you possibly can, with every one of your senses. Fill yourself with your outside world.

When you feel full, let a prayer of thanks flood out of your heart. Feel it moving out to the edges of your light in all directions. Feel the shifting perceptions in your own being.

Once you have thanked the Earth around your home, find a way to move these feelings into new action. An excellent journey to do, as part of this process, is a journey to the inner hunter to ask that you be led to the spirit of this land. Once you have met this spirit guardian, ask what it would *most* wish for you to do in support of the Earth. Ask for specific, concrete steps that you can actually take for this particular space.

The spirit of the land may ask you to find new ways to support plant growth without the use of chemicals. It may ask that you feed the birds, or put out food for the little ones. You may be asked to treat your waste differently. Any number of possibilities may be presented—and, best of all, you have learned them directly from the land itself. You have asked it what it needs most.

Check in with this spirit before changing the face of the Earth. Inquire about the best place to put your vegetable garden! Ask before cutting trees or building buildings. Always find out what impact your actions will have on the land, its plants, animals, water flows, and other concerns *before* you act.

For example, the spirits of place have been keeping track of weather a lot longer than the National Oceanic and Atmospheric Authority. Without first asking the spirit of place, can you be sure that you are situating your house on ground that is safe from flooding? I wonder how many "Storms of the Century" it will take before we remember to ask before taking action that could result in heartache?

There is a scientific basis for finding ways to communicate with the natural world. It was discovered recently that even trees emit a vibration that appears to be a form of communication. The existence of these "w-waves" was reported by physicist Ed Wagner in *Northwest Science.*[5] He noted that these vibrational emanations travel three feet per second through trees and fifteen feet per second through the air. He further noted that, when trees are cut, they produce an "alarm call" that is taken up by other surrounding trees.

---

[5] O. E. Wagner, "W-Waves and Plant Communication," *Northwest Science* (1989, 63:3), pp. 119–128.

Native peoples across the globe have always insisted on the sentience of all beings. It seems our science is beginning to prove that this is true. As sentient beings, creatures in nature communicate to each other just as we do. Using this knowledge, our entire lives may become an expression of respectful interaction. Just as we learn to interact with other humans in a nonhierarchical, mutually respectful manner, so too must we approach our relationship to *all* beings in this same light.

This is the foundational formula of sustainable living. As defined by the Gaia Educational Outreach Institute associated with the University of New Hampshire, planet-wide sustainable living requires four key elements: mindfulness, interdependence with the community of life, a seamless garment of time, and sustainable life skills and actions.

In other words, we must be aware, conscious, and respectful of all beings. We must examine all of our actions in the light of the future and remember that we are always in process. These are the very attributes of our inner hunter/gatherer!

When some of us open up to the larger ecological conditions, we may become despondent at the immensity of the task at hand. If you find yourself worrying along those lines, first get back into process.

When we find ourselves in worry or fear, it is usually because we are projecting an outcome. Even negative outcomes or projections are a sort of goal. If we see these projections of despair for what they are, we can more easily refocus our attentions to the present moment's task.

When these very human, and therefore inevitable, process-related interferences arise, stop, and then get into the grounded/expanded state. This usually helps release the tight grip of fear. If possible, take time to check in with the hunter to find out how he or she would handle the situation. (I find that the information gained from these journeys is usually something that breaks the mental stalemate!)

This brings us to a discussion of the role of the mind in this unfolding paradigm. The mind, when in service to the spirit, has the capacity to accelerate our evolution. On the other hand, when the mind (and its ego) is mired in the emotion of fear, it is capable of impeding much of what our hearts wish to accomplish.

Fear has so many forms. For many, it is the need to control; for others, it is an underlying anger or anxiety. Depression is another form often taken by this emotional and energetic sneak thief. But when we recognize these impediments to our process, we acquire ways to defeat their power. We can interrupt the cycle of interference with the grounded/expanded state, after which we can follow through by accessing our inner hunter, who teaches us how to "re-act" in fresh ways. As we continue to learn these new behavioral responses, we become more able to hold ourselves, the planet, and her creatures in a setting of deep compassion.

In every moment, the entirety of the cosmos is in a constant state of metamorphosis. Even though the scheme of the universe is vast, you only have to do *your* part. As each one of us interacts with our world differently, we are changing everything around us. We contribute more than we know.

This is illustrated by a marvelous concept called the Hundredth Monkey Phenomenon. Biologists on an island near Japan introduced sweet potatoes as a new component in the diet of the native monkeys. At first, the monkeys were hesitant to eat these freshly dug, and therefore dirty, potatoes. No other food available to them had ever before required washing! After some time had passed, a young female monkey carried the gritty potatoes to a stream, washed them, and began to feed. This female then taught her mother and her playmates to do the same. Her playmates then passed this new behavior on to their mothers as well. Initially, the only potato-washing monkeys were those who had been taught by their children. At some juncture, however, an extraordinary thing happened. The new behavior became universal, extending even to those monkeys who had never observed the washing behavior! This phenomenon has been referred to as the Hundredth Monkey Phenomenon. It supposes that, once a critical threshold of individuals in a population learns a behavior (or holds an idea), it becomes part of the collective intelligence.[6]

Since we, too, are primates, extending this behavioral ability to our own race isn't much of a stretch. By observing the people around us, we can see that when a group of individuals grasps a new concept, it can become part of a developing paradigm. In fact, isn't that how cultural perceptions develop? The question becomes: How many humans does it take to parallel the Hundredth Monkey Phenomenon? We can't yet be sure. However, this observation, this thought, can encourage us to move onward in our process. As the Buddha said, over 2,500 years ago:

---

[6] Lester W. Milbrath, *Envisioning a Sustainable Society* (Albany: State University of New York Press, 1989), p. 373.

We are what we think.
All that we are arises with our thoughts.
With our thoughts we make the world.[7]

Write down all that you perceive about your outdoor home. Ask yourself how it felt to send thanks to the land. The following questions will also help you think about your relationship to the land.

1. *How do I become a better steward of this land?*
2. *Please show me a vision of what this land was like 1,000 (or 10,000) years ago.*
3. *Please give me an experience of how all the beings on this land are connected.*
4. *How can I live in deeper balance with the Earth?*
5. *How is my body's inner ecology connected to the ecology of the Earth?*
6. *Please show me how my life changes the world.*

Conclusion

It is my profound wish that your inner hunter may give you the excitement in living and the peace of mind that my own wonderful hunter/gatherer provides. I have become deeply enriched through the magic of this spirit's gifts.

Since discovering this new way and working with this new paradigm, life and whatever life sends me is more joyfully experienced. In addition, I find that my interactions with other people and my environment flow more smoothly.

---

[7] Translation of Dhammapada, Pali Sources.

An energy of hope about the future and what it will bring all of us—and our planet—is growing. We are beginning to understand that, as each of us changes our lives in a positive direction, we contribute to this positive flow over the entire Earth. The tide of change is gathering momentum. Who knows which one of us will, in discovering the gifts of our inner hunter/gatherer, be the hundredth monkey?

Bibliography

Anderson, Myrdene, ed. *On Semiotic Modeling.* Berlin and New York: Mouton de Gruyter, 1991.

Andrews, Ted. *Animal Speak: The Spiritual and Magical Powers of Creatures Great and Small.* St. Paul, MN: Llewellyn Publications, 1995.

Bowles, Meg. *Blue Cosmos.* CD available from: Kumatone Records, New Fairfield, CT.

————. *Inner Space.* CD available from: Kumatone Records, New Fairfield, CT.

Burt, William H. *A Field Guide to the Mammals, North America North of Mexico.* (Peterson Field Guide #5) Boston and New York: Houghton Mifflin, 1980.

Castaneda, Carlos. *The Teachings of Don Juan: A Yaqui Way of Knowledge.* New York: Washington Square Press, 1968.

Chauvet, Jean-Marie, Eliette Brunel Deschamps, and Christian Hillaire. *Dawn of Art: The Chauvet Cave.* New York: Harry N. Abrams, 1996.

Colburn, Theo, Diane Dumanoski, and John Peterson Myers. *Our Stolen Future.* New York: Penguin Books, 1997.

Cowan, Eliot. *Plant Spirit Medicine.* Newberg, OR: Swan-Raven & Co., 1995.

Cowan, Tom. *Shamanism as Spiritual Practice for Daily Life.* Freedom, CA: The Crossing Press, 1996.

Eliot, Alexander. *The Universal Myths*. New York: New American Library (A Meridian Book), 1990 (reprint of 1976 original).

Elston, Catherine Feher. *Ravensong: A Natural and Fabulous History of Ravens and Crows*. Flagstaff, AZ: Northland Publishing, 1991.

Halifax, Joan. *Shaman, The Wounded Healer.* London and New York: Thames & Hudson, 1982.

———. *Shamanic Voices*. New York: E. P. Dutton, 1979.

Harner, Michael. *The Way of the Shaman*. New York: Harper & Row, 1980.

Izard, Carroll. *Human Emotions*. New York: Plenum Press, 1977.

Lawlor, Robert. *Voices of the First Day: Awakening in the Aboriginal Dreamtime*. Rochester, VT: Inner Traditions, 1991.

Milbrath, Lester W. *Envisioning a Sustainable Society*. Albany: State University of New York Press, 1989.

Mindel, Arnold. *The Shaman's Body*. New York: Harper-Collins, 1993.

Narby, Jeremy. *The Cosmic Serpent*. New York: Penguin/Putnam, 1998.

Northrup, Christiane. *Women's Bodies, Women's Wisdom*. New York: Bantam Books, 1994.

Rysdyk, Evelyn, with music by Meg Bowles. *Bedtime Stories for the New Human*. Audio cassette of shamanic stories available from: Spirit Passages, Yarmouth, ME.

Saunders, Nicholas, J. *Animal Spirits*. Boston: Little, Brown and Company (Living Wisdom Series), 1995.

Shepherd, Paul. *The Sacred Paw: The Bear in Nature, Myth and Literature*. London and New York: Arkana (Penguin Group), 1985.

Soule, Deb. *The Roots of Healing: A Woman's Book of Herbs*. New York: Citadel Press/Carol Publishing Group, 1995.

Swan, James A. *Nature as Teacher and Healer*. New York: Villard Books (Random House), 1992.

Vitebsky, Piers. *The Shaman*. Boston: Little Brown, 1995.

Weil, Andrew. *Natural Health, Natural Medicine*. Boston: Houghton Mifflin Company, 1990.

Index

Evelyn Rysdyk is a graduate of the Foundation for Shamanic Studies three-year program, and had the privilege of studying with indigenous teachers including the late Mikail Duvan, the last remaining male shaman of the Ulchi People of Southeastern Siberia.

She is an internationally recognized artist, author, and shamanic practitioner who enjoys life most when she is able to combine her spiritual and artistic lives, honoring the sacredness of all things. Her paintings and works in silver are in private collections throughout Europe, Canada, China, and Russia, as well as across the United States. An example of the author's artistic work adorns the cover of this book. This piece is called "Living in the Magic," and is available as a limited edition print from Spirit Passages.

Ms. Rysdyk co-founded Spirit Passages, a private shamanic teaching and healing practice, with C. Allie Knowlton, MSW, in 1992. It was founded to provide individuals with the tools to become conscious participants in their healing, wellness, and spiritual evolution. The author can be contacted at Spirit Passages for additional information, including information about her art and audio cassette:

Spirit Passages
P.O. Box 426
Yarmouth, ME 04096